Please return/renew this item by the last date shown.
Herefordshire Libraries

VERY REPITITIOUS – NOT AS
FUNNY AS HE THINKS

Talk to the Tail

Talk to the Tail

Adventures in Cat Ownership
and Beyond

TOM COX

**SIMON &
SCHUSTER**

London · New York · Sydney · Toronto

A CBS COMPANY

First published in Great Britain by Simon & Schuster UK Ltd, 2011
A CBS COMPANY

Copyright © 2011 by Tom Cox

A CIP catalogue for this book is
available from the British Library.

ISBN: 978-1-84737-817-0

Typeset by M Rules
Printed in the UK by CPI Mackays, Chatham ME5 8TD

In memory of Jeanne Francis, and Kiffer

Acknowledgements

A big thanks to those who also served: Angela Herlihy, Colin Midson, Simon Trewin, Ariella Feiner, Vicky Halls, Hannah Lynch, Henry Lynch, Daniel Carway, Louise Marshall, Michael Cox, Jo Cox, Alex German, Cassie Campbell, Ian Allen, Jackie Morris, Max, the Ginger Army and The People Sheep.

'That's supposed to be a fact, that the question mark is originally from an Egyptian hieroglyph that signified a cat walking away. You know, it's the tail. And the symbol meant – well, whatever it is when they're ignoring you.' – Christopher Walken, 'What I've Learned', American *Esquire* magazine, June 2009

'If animals could speak, the dog would be a blundering outspoken fellow, but the cat would have the rare grace of never saying a word too much.' – Mark Twain

'A bear doesn't go to sleep thinking, "I wasn't really a very good bear today." They are just 100 per cent bear, whereas human beings feel we're not 100 per cent human. We're constantly striving towards something, to some fulfilment.' – Stephen Fry

'It's dog eat dog, and cat eat mouse, you can rag mama rag all over my house.' – The Band, 'Rag Mama Rag'

Contents

War Baby

For most of the average week, my home town of East Mendleham is a quiet sort of place. Often, I will go for as many as six days without hearing any sound more vociferous drifting from the centre of the town than that of an old man swearing encouragingly at some ducks as they take his bread, or an elderly covers group on the park bandstand. This is the standard innocuous backing track of a British market town: the distant cry of an eccentric, some mildly confused birdlife, and a version of 'That'll Be the Day' drifting on the breeze, no less benign for the this-could-actually-*be*-the-day tension injected into its lyrics by its infirm practitioners. But from about seven o'clock on a Friday to about three o'clock on Saturday morning, East Mendleham, like many other British market towns, comes alive. If you're on the street during this period, what you will essentially be experiencing is a simulation of a Wild West frontier settlement, with Subarus instead of horses. Tyres screech, arguments are settled in public, primeval mating rituals abound, and the energy of the week is burned off in a blaze of pent-up, Stella Artois-swigging glory.

I'm old enough now to look at this philosophically. It still isn't all that long ago that I lived in a London flat where, every Wednesday evening, at 9 pm on the dot, a young couple would stand an inch from my bedroom window, arguing loudly about whether or not their baby was 'a Paki': the same flat where Tuesday night could be relied upon to be Ladies' Night. And what I mean by Ladies' Night, in this case, is Lady From The Flat Upstairs Having Sex Loudly To Primal Scream's *Screamadelica* Album Night. It's even less long since I lived in a terraced house where the framework would shake on a near 24-hour basis from the 'rehearsals' of the empty-eyed DJ next door and the barks of his mum's giant, unhappy dog. Thankfully, the walls of my house are now all my own, and one night of drunken people burning off steam outside my house seems a small price to pay for six days of peace.

This is not to say, however, that those walls always feel like adequate protection. I have to confess that, until the summer of 2007, I'd never given any great thought to what it would be like to have three men attack your house with pruning shears at three on a Saturday morning, but, if I had, I'm sure I would not have been able to imagine the terrifying onslaught of industrial noise involved. It was such a relief to look outside and discover that the men in question were only trying to steal the lead flashing off the front of the house, and not performing a renovation to turn it into their own personal drinking establishment. I half wanted to thank them. What I did instead was ask them what the jolly heck they were doing (although, now I really think about it, perhaps I didn't quite put it in those terms). In response, they immediately slunk off. I felt quite brave and pleased with myself, for about twenty minutes, until I realised they'd just gone to get some bigger pairs of secateurs in order to do the job more successfully, and my wife Dee and I decided to put the matter in the – on this occasion – very capable hands of the police. This occurred only a week before we were paid a visit by two sunken-cheeked gentlemen who, when questioned by me regarding the precise vagaries of why they were perched on my wheelie bin, trying to hoist themselves over the fence leading to my garden, said unconvincingly, 'We're not trying to rob you, mate, honest!'

To be fair, there was a whole Friday's respite between that and my car getting broken into. Nonetheless, given the preceding events, it was probably only natural that, two Fridays later, when Dee woke me up at 3 am and announced, 'There's someone in the bedroom,' I did what any other self-respecting male would do when called to defend his domestic realm and those within it: I stood up, naked and fearless, grabbed a plastic watering can, and got ready to fight for everything I held dear.

I'd experienced the aftermath of two burglaries before, back when I lived with my parents, but on neither occasion was I in the house when they took place. Now, I listened hard for movement, feeling genuinely in danger of suffocating from the silence. Wherever the intruder was, he remained icily still. At least, I assumed it was a he. A female reader of the blog I write about my cats had recently emailed me, threatening to move her stuff and her cats into my and Dee's place. She was just joking – wasn't she? I froze, keeping my breathing to a bare minimum, and allowing my eyes to become accustomed to the dark. Was that a human-sized lump behind the curtains?

This was one of those moments nervously dreaded by any adult who has worked hard all their life to build something to protect. You pictured it on your darkest nights, but you didn't believe it would really happen to you.

'*Where?*' I tried to hiss and shape the word in a manner that would somehow achieve the impossible: sending it across to Dee, without it being intercepted by the ears of the intruder.

I thought of the infamous farmer from my home county who had shot the two youths who'd broken into his house a few years ago. People called him a crank, a bloodthirsty hick, but placed in the same situation, I now knew those people's take on the situation would be different. 'You don't think Charlton Heston and his National Rifle Association buddies are so silly now, do you?' said a little demon voice in my head, as I pointed the plastic spout of my weapon into the darkness.

In retrospect, I could have been better-armed – not reaching immediately for the ceramic bedside lamp was already beginning to seem like a glaring oversight, and even the paperback on the table next to it would have been a distinct improvement – but the watering can had been the first thing I'd seen, and now I had it, the important thing was to commit without undue hesitation.

'*Under the bed,*' said Dee.

'You're sodding kidding me?' I said, considerably louder.

'No. Just leave him. He can go out in the morning.'

Had my wife lost her mind? Was she suggesting that I not only ignore the fact that a strange man – maybe more than one strange man – had broken into our house, but that I blithely let him get on with his business? I looked at her in a whole new way, shadowy figure that she was, propped up on her pillow. Maybe she had planned this entire operation. I had been living with a stranger for seven years, and now I was going to pay the ultimate price for my trust and naivety!

'Come back to bed.'

Thinking 'To hell with it!' and that I might as well look my fate right in the eye as I accepted it, I turned on the light. We'd now stopped whispering, and if there had been a burglar or psychopath in the room with us, he would have had an insurmountable upper hand in carrying out whatever bodily harm he had planned. Fortunately, though, it was clear from the way he emerged from his hiding place, bounded up onto the duvet, Tigger-style, and flopped moronically on his back, that Pablo would happily put senseless violence to one side. Or at least that he would defer it for the time being, on the condition that he could find a willing servant to scruff up his chest fur in his favourite, vigorous manner.

'Sometimes,' I said, as an ocean of tension drained from my body, 'I wonder if, on the whole, it might be less confusing for all concerned if we stopped referring to our cats as "someone".'

I have lived in several homes that creak with history, but the light, airy, early 1960s building where I currently reside is not one of them. Although I can't state this as a fact, I feel fairly certain in saying that nobody has ever died in here. It's just not that kind of house. Like a bouncy castle or a Spice Girls video, it's one of those environments that tend to actively discourage thought of the supernatural. That said, on a Friday night, it clicks and vibrates with mysterious sounds. Objects skitter across the floor, unbidden. Alien voices echo through its air pockets.

'Darrrrrr-rrr-en, llll-llll-eavvve it. It's nott-tt worth it . . .
He's just a looo-oooo-ser . . .'

And every so often, a banshee-like wailing can be heard
emanating from the region of the staircase.

'Meeeea-wa-wa-wa-wa!'

I'm sure that those who live with an actual ghost would
claim to have it far worse. The creeping feeling of being
unwelcome in your own home. The heavy atmosphere. The
sudden, unexplainable drops in temperature. But I'm not so
convinced. What, when it comes right down to it, is the
worst a spectre can do? Break a couple of antique vases?
Open and close a couple of doors with the force of its sheer
unresolved ancient discontentment? Big deal. Does a ghost
get high on pills and try to steal some lead from your house?
No. It would consider such an activity uncouth. There are
some seriously chilling manifestations of the afterlife in the
stories of M.R. James and Edgar Allan Poe, but, for all their
malice, the chances of them getting drunk, pilfering a plant
pot and dropping it from a great height on a nearby duck's
nest 'for a laugh' seem quite slim.

No doubt, were I to live in a house with its own headless
horsemen legend, it could be a bit of a bind at times, what
with the midnight whinnying and the repeat decapitations,
but at least he'd be scrupulously clean. Say what you like
about headless horsemen's horses, you don't find them
coming into your bedroom at night when it's been raining,
expecting to be dried off and soiling your duvet with their
hoof marks.

There's also a pleasing lack of ambiguity about ghosts.
Once you've established you have a supernatural force in
residence and you hear a bump in the night, at least you
can say, 'Oh, that'll only be the Old Man Who Watches

The Graveyard, searching for his murdered wife's hair again.' You're not sitting up for hours on end wondering, 'Was that a speed freak attempting to get in through my front door, or just a mouse's cranium being batted against a skirting board?'

Living with several cats, in a British market town, in a house built into a hill, by the main route to and from the local dispensers of alcoholic beverages – a B road that's one of the busiest in East Mendleham, and which souped-up Peugeots and Subarus speed down on a Friday night – I am doomed never to be so certain. I can't think of any obvious reason my cats have decided to make their weekly Party Night coincide with that of the human population of East Mendleham. Each one of the furry schemers in my house has his or her clandestine double life, but I find it hard to believe that any of these would extend to a nine-to-five job working in a call centre, and its concomitant end-of-week stress-relief session.

It's not as if it gets to Friday afternoon and the six of them think, 'You know what? I'm really pooped from five days of sleeping on the sofa, repeatedly cleaning my bottom and having my every whim catered for. What I really need to do is *unwind*.' Nonetheless, the end of their working week is the time they choose to slaughter more voles, the night when they meow the loudest, the night when their need to wander and fight and carouse seems most unquenchable.

Even if I didn't have cats, Friday would still be my Worry Night, but the commotion they make and their vulnerable proximity to other nearby commotion heightens my concern. I stay vigilant for much the same reason that I will never go to sleep on an aeroplane: to give myself an all-important illusion of control. This is not just about people breaking in, it's about feeling that, by the mere act of being awake, I can stop my cats getting hit by a car.

I live in an odd building – a place with a layout so disorientating that a few years ago, when Dee and I were thinking of selling it, a prospective buyer tried to leave via a cupboard. Known as the Upside Down House, and erected flush up to one of the approximate four hills in South Norfolk, most of its rooms are actually underground and somewhat cavelike. Because the main bedroom is underneath the parking space, it's also underneath the seven-foot fence Dee and I installed in a despairing attempt to stop The Bear and Shipley from getting to the road from the garden. I hear the dull thud of their landings on the other side of the fence, and sometimes race upstairs to meet them before they get to the road. Sometimes, I'll look under my car and see The Bear's bright, incensed eyes staring back at me. Other times, I'll catch Shipley before he has made his kamikaze dash, and he will greet me at the front door with a volley of questions, which I'll do my best to answer:

'What are you doing up here?! You're not supposed to be up here at this time of night! This is a different door to the one I normally come through. It's not the regular door! That excites me! Why does it excite me?'

'Well, it's technically my house, so I can go where I like, but I'm up here primarily because I was worried about you. You're going to come in now, aren't you, and then, just as I've settled back down and closed my eyes, you're going to go out again, and go back over the fence.'

'Yes, of course I am. Mainly because I'm a cat, and therefore inherently stubborn.'

'Also, where's that reflective collar I bought you?'

'I ditched it. Do I look like the kind of soppy twit who

would be seen dead wearing baby blue and glitter? What do you think I am, a sodding Burmese?"

There are a number of quiet hours on a Friday, following the moment when the final few locals bring their arguments to a drooling, incoherent impasse and stumble off the wall at the front of the house, but these come to an end when Shipley and Ralph announce their arrivals back from their midnight wanders.

When I enter a house, I tend to do so with decorum and humility, not expecting congratulations. But for Shipley, the mere act of safe passage through a miniature door is an achievement to be greeted with a fanfare halfway between what one might expect on the hometown leg of a sell-out stand-up comedy tour and a victorious Olympic run.

Originally, Shipley was very much an 'extra' cat: a runtish black goblin whose puckish energy stood out, prompting me to beg Dee to be able to take him home with his brothers Ralph and Brewer, (sadly no longer with us.) To his credit, that first night he managed to very impressively stifle his gobby, all-consuming need to be the centre of attention every second of every day, snuggling down quietly at the end of the bed as Dee and I slept with Brewer and Ralph respectively curled up in the crook of our arms. This was his one concession to good manners, before making it perfectly clear that, from that day on, his entire existence would require a soundtrack, of which he would be the writer, arranger and singer. The voice came first, a sort of *meeyap* that seemed to belong only one third to a cat, with the other two thirds split between a petulant lapdog and the kind of overzealous spider monkey who, as you admired it at the zoo, might run off up a tree with your purse. This was soon followed by a growth spurt leading to obstinate sinewiness that somehow seemed to complement the noises emerging from it.

Shipley looks muscular, but retains the appearance of a slim cat, and friends who visit gasp as they pick him up. 'What weighs so much?' they wonder. The answer, I would wager, is the sheer heft of self-belief. I've had short, reedy school-friends in the past who've seemed to will themselves into muscular adulthood, but Shipley is the first cat I've known to achieve something similar.

The door to the main bedroom of my house is a heavy one, fitted a little too close to the carpet beneath it. Even for a human, it takes a bit of a shove to open, and for most felines it's a lost cause, but for Shipley, at the crack of dawn, it is no obstacle. Since I don't have a camera set up in my living room, I have no actual evidence of how he goes about getting it open, but I like to picture a scenario involving a miniature stepladder and a ten-inch battering ram fashioned from a long-out-of-date courgette. You might have thought after going to such an effort, he would want to make the most of the ample comforts of the room, but Shipley's visits are flying ones: brief windows in his schedule where I am invited to join him in revelling in his own magnificence, before he leaves for more pressing appointments.

'It's me! I'm here!' he will say, upon getting the door open, and quickly hiding the courgette and the stepladder before I get the chance to see them.

'That's nice,' I will say blearily. 'Very much like this time last morning, in fact.'

'I have rain on my back!'

'And in what way is that my problem?'

'It's your sodding problem because you know that if you

don't wipe it off in the next seven seconds I'm going to smear my muddy paws all over the duvet, and if that still doesn't work, I'm going to start shredding the magazines by your bedside or find a bit of really soft flesh on your arm and pinch it between my front teeth until you do what I say.'

'Has it occurred to you what kind of long-term effects it can have on people's sleep pattern, when every morning, between five and six-thirty, they have cats shouting in their faces?'

'No, that has never occurred to me. I have absolutely no concept of The Long Term or The Big Picture. I live entirely in the moment, and think exclusively about my own needs, on a minute-by-minute basis. Because of this, I will always be much happier than you. Now shut the hell up and stroke this wet shit off my back.'

'Is it normal to be sworn at by a cat? I'm sure that's not normal. Do ordinary people's ordinary cats do that? I feel sure they don't, you know. Could I at least have some kind of cuddle, since you're here?'

'You know what? I would love to, but I'm just a bit worried about that issue of *Private Eye* that's been left in the living room. I'm not quite happy with Gordon Brown's face on the cover, and would like to rip into it with my teeth. Best not leave it much longer, for fear it annoys someone. Sorry, but you know how it is.'

Each of my cats has spent time cultivating their own specialist method for waking me up. There was, for example, the two-month period where, every day, between 6.30 and 7 am, Bootsy would manage to locate my favourite ring – which I always take off at night – on my bedside table, and bat it into the adjacent wastepaper basket. A more distanced onlooker might suggest that this was simply a demonstration of Bootsy's love for shiny objects, which is a valid theory – she's always had expensive taste – but the fact that she immediately lost interest in the ring every time my attention was roused suggests there was always more to it.

Then there's Janet, whose wake-up calls employ the infamous The Nice Cat/Stinky Cat method, first practised by felines in ancient Egypt who were worried about not getting the attention that, as would-be gods, they felt they deserved. First, he will burrow his head under the duvet and press his ice-cold nose into one of my feet. To be on the receiving end of this tactical manoeuvre is far from unpleasant, but, should it fail to rouse me, he will bring out the big guns, hauling his great hulking bottom up onto the bed and cleaning it two inches from my face. The other symptom of this, besides me wanting to get as far away from the bed as quickly as possible, is that, going on the rule of Simulslurp, any other cat in the room will also start cleaning its bottom at the same time. Soon, Shipley will invariably arrive, and then Ralph too, burrowing into his own rear in a manner that, were it to get any more thorough, could put him in severe danger of re-eating the previous day's shrew. This will often lead to a kind of 'arse chorus', which, if it wasn't for the fact that I feel sure someone else has done it already, I might have filmed and put on YouTube by now.

But it's always Ralph and Shipley who are most adamant about having their needs met. I do not think of myself as my cats' 'father', but since these are the only two cats that didn't get time to be significantly moulded by another owner before coming into my care, I find it hard not to view their behaviour as a sign of my parental shortcomings. They are milksops: toughnuts in one way, entirely needy in another. Unlike Shipley, Ralph does not have the ingenuity to open the bedroom door, instead choosing to howl his own name to get my attention. I've asked him lots of questions about the reasons for this over the years, ranging from 'Have you sustained a debilitating leg injury?' all the way to 'Did you have that dream about being mocked by a stoat again?' but he's never really come up with an answer more elucidatory than 'Raaaaaaaeeeeaaalph!'

Ralph has always been a bit of a nighttime howler, and his low spells in hot weather long ago led me to conclude that he suffers from a summertime version of Seasonal Affective Disorder, but in the late summer of 2007, not long after the men attacked the house with the gardening implements, the frequency of his vocal pronouncements of his name and the proximity of them to Dee's and my sleeping quarters and the street above made them an extra cause for concern.

In an age when cats seem to be gradually taking over the Internet, one might assume that, using half-decent research skills, it might be possible to find out a diagnosis for any kind of curious feline behaviour online within a matter of seconds. However, having Googled 'your tabby' 'a' 'becomes' 'when' and 'massive prat' I found nothing. Dee's suggestion was that his unease could be down to the all-white, fluffy cat we sometimes saw flicking her tail about on the stairs leading to the back garden, and had christened The Whore. But, as astute as Dee is on 99 per cent of other-worldly matters, she's always had a weak spot when it comes to second-guessing Ralph's woes, going right back to his kittenhood, before we realised he was a boy, when she mistook his midnight howls for mating calls.

From what I could see, the only negative thing you could say about The Whore was that she had an unusually flicky, flirty tail. From my limited knowledge of catiquette, this hardly seemed a crime worth meowling about around the neighbourhood, stating your identity at the top of your voice. It wasn't as if she'd invited one of her mates in for a fight behind our living room curtains, as a giant neighbourhood tabby had done in the summer of 2002.[1]

If we were honest, the two of us probably knew what the problem was quite early on, and, by looking for other causes, and scapecats such as The Whore, were merely trying to find a way not to face up to it.

In the past, our cats had always got on with one another fairly well. Certainly, there was the annual punch-up between Ralph and Shipley where Ralph would pound Shipley's head against the concrete patio just to confirm who was still Top Cat, or those moments where Shipley would sneak up onto the bed and play the timeless game of 'Clappy Paws' with The Bear's inert, sleeping form, or that occasion that Bootsy knocked The Bear flying against the patio doors with one of her tiny, legendary right hooks. But this was ultimately play fighting, with no serious grudges behind it. For a while, I'd convinced myself that the stand-offs between Ralph and Pablo fitted into a similar category. I suppose, though, when one of your cats pounces on one of your other cats with such force that he snaps your cat flap door off twice in one week, you have to accept that you might be dealing with a slightly more serious problem.

Before he came to us, Pablo had been living as one of dozens of feral cats in a giant, abandoned house, where he would regularly impregnate various close members of his family. I picture it as a kind of cat version of a 1960s hippie

---

[1] This had been a pain at the time, but over the years I'd come to miss it.

commune, except with a slightly less overpowering smell of urine. His background meant he came to us with three fundamental needs: a) to eat as much food as felinely possible; b) to make friends with any other cat in the vicinity; and c) to dry hump something soft at least once daily. Bootsy provided a willing outlet for needs b) and c) and Dee and I did our best to satisfy need a), but the other cats remained sceptical of the new wiry ginger simpleton in their midst. To an intellectually superior cat, such as The Bear, Pablo's condition presented no problem: Pablo did not even feature on The Bear's radar. But to a narcissistic, troubled, yet not particularly bright cat such as Ralph, the ginger newcomer's outlook on life must have seemed nigglingly simple. This seemed to me to be more of a war of species than anything else: the eternal battle between the sunny ginger and the tortured tabby. That was my theory, anyway. But one thing was for certain: as summer turned into autumn, Ralph was feeling threatened by Pablo in an additional, more physical way.

In 2007, when friends would ask me how many cats I had, I would tell them 'six', but I was actually lying – I had seven. It was just that all seven never lived in the house at the same time. There was The Bear, Shipley, Janet, Ralph and Bootsy, and Summer Pablo. Then, around September each year, Summer Pablo would vanish to be replaced by another cat, known as Winter Pablo. Winter Pablo was ginger, had many of the same habits of Summer Pablo, and cultivated a similarly intellectually challenged look by leaving his tongue permanently protruding from his mouth, but that was pretty much where the resemblance ended. I tend to chalk up Pablo's vast, terrifying accrual of winter weight to his feralness, but I've never known another cat to do it in such exaggerated fashion. It must have been disturbing, being Ralph, the joint biggest of all my cats, to suddenly see one of your skinnier contemporaries transform himself into a giant red pom-pom as the weather got colder.

Did Ralph actually think it was another ginger cat altogether – equally as much of an annoying bum onion as the other one, but even fatter – coming in through the cat flap? Maybe an out-and-out moron like my second oldest cat, Janet, might have made that mistake, but I credited Ralph with more intelligence. Although maybe not enough intelligence to remember that Pablo's weight gain had occurred the previous two winters as well and, come March, Summer Pablo would begin to return.

So what was responsible for tipping the balance and creating Ralph's vendetta? Now, as I happened upon the pair of them in mid-scrap, I noticed a new intensity to their wrangling. In the human world, to get two individuals at such loggerheads, one of them would have probably had to have slept with the other's spouse, stolen their job, or taken out a hit on a close member of their family. But for Ralph and Pablo, all these possibilities seemed moot, apart from maybe the first, and I was certain Ralph had no real romantic, or dry hump-based, designs on Bootsy, nor Pablo on the sheepskin rug draped across the back of the living room sofa that Ralph often turned to for physical comfort in his more carnal moments. The couple of times Pablo had had a tentative go on the sheepskin, it had only made him sneeze.

I'd initially thought that what we were dealing with here was a simple aggressor–victim situation, with Ralph in the aggressor role, but it soon became apparent that Pablo's happy-go-lucky veneer was beginning to crack. Pablo might have been a big soft pom-pom when bounding onto the bed and asking to have his chest scruffed, but he was also one with scalpel-deadly talons. I found this to my cost one day, when I reached through the cat flap tunnel and readjusted the door, only for Pablo to mistake my hand for Ralph and punish it accordingly.[2]

Soon, the exits and corners of the house became places of fiery red trepidation for Ralph. The top of the small staircase leading from the bottom floor was a particular danger point. Once, I arrived here to find Ralph and Pablo both simultaneously suspended upside down, in mid-air, three feet off the ground. From what I could work out, no string, rope or pulley system was in place. It was my usual habit to hurl myself in between them during their scraps, but this time I held back just momentarily, unable to stop myself admiring the ballet of the performance. I will not be persuaded that a full three seconds didn't elapse before both their heads hit the ground. It was like something from *The Matrix*, the main exceptions being that, post-fight, characters from *The Matrix* don't a) violently shed fur all over the floor and b) go and sulk behind the sofa.

There was always far more fur to clean up in the aftermath of Ralph and Pablo's tussles than there was following the recreational wrestling bouts between Janet and Shipley. If I'd had the foresight to save the stuff, it probably would have only taken about half a dozen fights before I had enough to make a whole new cat: a tabby-ginger half-breed

---

[2] The bleeding stopped after a couple of hours, and I suppose I could forgive him the error: my hands, while not remotely tabby, are quite oversensitive and narcissistic.

named Rablo who might go forth and spread peace, putting an end to racial tension in the cat universe once and for all.

But it seems doubtful Rablo would have succeeded where 'mellowing' Feliway plug-ins, valerian drops and pep talks had not. My own interventions certainly weren't doing much good either. Perhaps the most calamitous of them was the occasion when, in whisking Pablo out from Ralph's reach and closing the bedroom door, being careful not to shut it on Pablo's tail, I suddenly realised I was holding a furry ginger air raid alarm whose off switch I could not locate. I've never heard such a bloodcurdling sound coming from a cat and an interminable twenty seconds went by before I realised that it was not a continuation of Pablo's battle cry I was hearing but his way of informing me that, in going to such an attempt not to trap his tail in the door, I'd trapped it in the hinge of the door instead. It took me quite some time to apologise for that one, with the extensive use of pâté – always a dangerous move with Pablo, a cat who, once given a taste, can never quite be convinced that a human is incapable of producing spreadable paste on demand.

Working from home takes strict discipline. That discipline can easily be fractured when a person spends half his day serving as a peacemaker between his cats. Now, with Dee out at her new job at a local horse charity, I found myself devoting large amounts of time to trying to placate Ralph and Pablo and soothe their bruised egos. Ralph is a cat who can twist his way inside your chest like a rusty screwdriver with his repertoire of hurt looks, and I found myself being particularly diligent to make sure his feelings weren't damaged. Outsiders might think the logical thing to do, having run for the doorbell, fallen over on the stairs, lightly trodden on your cat, bruised your shin and scraped a chunk of skin off the palm of your hand, would be to attempt to stop the courier driving off with the package containing the DVD you need to review in your newspaper column that afternoon, or sit down and recover with a calming cup of tea. Instead, I chose a third option: chase after the cat in question, telling him how profusely sorry you are, and promising never to do it again, not once considering that it might be his own stupid fault for sitting on the stairs in the first place.

Sometimes, as I found myself singing my alternative version of Billy Joel's 'Vienna' to Pablo ('Slow down/You ginger cat/You're so ambitious for a . . . ginger cat') and Ralph walked into the room, I would quickly switch to 'Tabby Lover', a rewrite of Phil Collins' and Philip Bailey's 1985 chart-topping duet 'Easy Lover' that I would be the first to admit needed some work ('He's a tabby lover/He'll do a fart and you won't hear it'). 'Pablo's coat is looking extremely plush today,' I'd say to Dee, who would tighten her lips and point with her eyes at Ralph, sitting behind me on his sheepskin lover, causing me to add, '. . . And then there's Ralph's sideburns. Have you seen how thick they are right now? Magnificent!' It would probably be going too far to say I got more careful about eating oranges and carrots while Ralph was around, but I won't deny that it crossed my mind.

I spent a lot of time checking Pablo was okay too, but it seemed clear that the ginger was slowly getting the upper hand. If Ralph could have backed down, he probably would have, but the battle had gone beyond that stage – there was too much pride at stake. Shipley joined in the goading of Pablo occasionally, but that was clearly for his own amusement. There was no amusement about this for Ralph or

Pablo by now: the battle had progressed somewhere newly senseless. But isn't that always the way with war? That the individuals most liable to get hurt by it can no longer remember what they're fighting for?

Ralph began to avoid the cat flap altogether, instead standing for periods of up to three hours outside the bedroom window, shouting. 'Raaalph!' he would howl, and I would sit up in bed, debating whether to let him in and encourage his neediness or attempt to sleep through it. 'I yam Raaalph!' he would sometimes add after half an hour or so, just in case we'd been left in any doubt about exactly who it might be out there, acting like an absolute tool.

'Leave him,' said Dee. 'If you let him in, he'll realise that he's got you wrapped around his little finger, and he'll never come in through the cat flap ever again.'

I could see the logic of her advice, but I had two problems with it. Firstly, Ralph didn't actually have a little finger; but he did have paws, and it did not take much for me to conjure up the image of one of these paws, cold and forlorn, scraping against the window of a next-door neighbour's kitchen window, asking for love, having finally given up on me.

Secondly, I knew the advice was coming from a somnolent being of rare powers. I only had to think back to one of our first arguments as a domestic couple to remember this. I forget what the argument was about now, and I'm pretty sure it wasn't cleaning, but it ended with Dee falling asleep and me having the brainwave that, if I scrubbed, hoovered and dusted the flat from top to bottom, it would somehow prove that I was right about everything in the entire universe, for ever. Whatever the warped logic that made me think this, my plan clearly didn't work, as Dee slept soundly through my vacuuming, and the main upshots were that I had time to realise I was wrong about whatever we were arguing about, and she woke up, well rested, to a blissfully clean flat. I've learned since then that she can sleep through louder sounds than the one a vacuum cleaner makes when it's on full power three feet from your head, so, even though I applauded her pragmatism and took into account her wisdom, I had to also take into account that the sound of hopped-up, hyper-sensitive cats has never disturbed her. (The hopped-up, hyper-sensitive cats seem to know this too, which is why they have never bothered to try to wake her up, knowing that there is someone far more gullible and malleable nearby.)

Suggestions flooded in from family and acquaintances close and distant about what to do about the problem with Ralph and the cat door. My friend Vicky, who works as a cat behaviourist, echoed Dee's suggestion that a second cat flap might be in order. But Dee's bird-loving, feline-disliking mum, Oriole, disagreed. 'It seems like a lot of bother, and quite expensive. Wouldn't it be easier to just get rid of all your cats? You probably won't miss them in the long run.' A more novel, if still impractical, suggestion came from my friend Liz, who is not only very good at sorting out cat problems, but pretty good at sorting computer problems too. 'Have you tried letting him in and out again?' she asked.

When I suggested inviting Vicky to the house to meet the cats, Dee seemed apprehensive. 'But she'll find us out, and tell us we're terrible owners.'

'Yes, well, I suppose it might be an idea to take the padlock off the airing cupboard and let Bootsy out before she comes.'

'You know what I mean. She *knows* stuff.'

Vicky calls herself a cat behaviour counsellor, and has also been referred to as a 'cat shrink' and – not her personal favourite, this – 'pussy doctor'. If you were someone who visited up to 250 different cat owners' homes a year it would be forgivable if you started not just to think like a cat but to incorporate a repertoire of growls, purrs and disdainful sniffs into everyday discourse. However, the last thing you think upon meeting Vicky is 'here's a person who probably owns kitten-faced place mats'.

Arriving at the house in a sports car so low-riding it had trouble climbing the not particularly steep ramp onto my driveway, she did not exude cattishness and, if anything, seemed more likely to be mistaken for a Labrador owner. She knows cats better than anyone I know, but only owns one, and, much as she loves Mangus, her Devon Rex, she is not afraid to slag her off. 'She can be a bit clingy sometimes,' she told me, placing a leather bag on the living room floor. 'And, you know, I'm not really that big a fan of pedigrees. I prefer moggies.'

There was something about the leather bag that didn't quite fit in with the sharp business-lady attire and the fast car, but I couldn't quite put my finger on it. Actually, it would probably be more accurate to say I was slightly *afraid* to put my finger on it, for fear of what might end up on my finger. The last time I'd come across a piece of hand luggage so weathered and aromatic of a full and varied life was my old school bag, shortly after I'd made the misguided decision to use it to transport a chicken curry back on the school bus after a Home Economics class.

'It's a bit grungy, I know,' said Vicky. She told me she had no idea exactly what combination of various different types of catnip, catmint and valerian had given it its magic, but knew it worked, and that she could not recreate it if she tried. 'If any problems are there, this tends to bring them to the surface,' she said.

As if on cue, Shipley appeared and plunged snout-first into the bag's heady depths, while Bootsy appeared right behind him, and plunged snout-first into the heady depths of Shipley. Almost instantly, from the floor below, we heard the crash of the cat flap and a 'SCREEEOOW' noise and rushed to the window to see Pablo's retreating form. A moment later, Ralph appeared, sporting an expression that seemed to speak of manifold grievances, chief among them possibly being 'someone has stolen my mittens'.

'They have these scraps about four times a day at the moment,' I told Vicky.

'Sometimes it's good if they fight,' said Vicky. 'It means it's all out in the open. The big worry is when they internalise their problems.'

This was an unexpected piece of wisdom, and it led me to ponder a whole set of problems I hadn't even imagined, then thank my lucky stars I wasn't experiencing them. Okay, so it was a shame that Pablo sometimes clawed Ralph's bottom so viciously he removed a chunk of fur big enough to wear as a tabby war bonnet, but at least he wasn't putting his foe down with sarcasm, pretend pleasantries and backhanded compliments.

'He's forgotten to put his tongue back in,' said Vicky, pointing towards Pablo. 'I love it when they do that.'

I could have told her the truth, which was that, in Pablo's case, this wasn't an oversight so much as a permanent default setting, but I thought better of it. I was anxious that my cats didn't all come across as complete morons, and I sensed that Shipley had already gone past the point of no redemption in that respect. By now, only his legs were visible above the top of the bag. I had no idea what sort of hedonistic pleasures he'd found in there, but I couldn't help thinking of the famous scene in the movie *Trainspotting*, where Ewan McGregor puts his head into a toilet and finds that the bowl suddenly expands into a magical junkie's swimming pool.

It was a full hour before Vicky found the first urine stain. 'It's just a little spotting, nothing much,' she said, examining the stair rail near where Ralph and Pablo had many of their tussles, then recalled the time she leaned on a partition wall in a client's house that was so rotted with feline effluence that her hand went through and out the other side. She called our house a 'harmonious feline set-up' and recommended once again, that Ralph and Pablo might be mollified by adding an extra cat flap.

I couldn't tell if, being a friend, Vicky was quite giving it to me straight. I also realised that 'harmony' was relative in this case: her recent clients included a man whose cat had seriously injured his foreskin during a 'waggling incident' and a woman who managed to tell her within twenty seconds of their first meeting that she'd known her cat in seven previous lives and had a multiple personality disorder, while also hinting that her late father was a murderer. However, I did notice that there was a palpable change of mood in the aftermath of her visit.

Like most cats, mine spent the majority of their lives sleeping, but this was the first time I could recall my house having the full-on feel of a feline opium den. What had Vicky done to the six of them? There'd been the magic bag, of course, and the various ailing, well-loved toys that she later produced from it – an extremely popular mouse and octopus among them. Or was it a pig and a spider? The effects of years of toothmarks and drool had made it a little hard to tell.

You wouldn't call Vicky a Cat Whisperer. She hadn't sat down with them at any point for a 'quiet word' or pinched their necks and made hissing sounds when they started to misbehave. But even while she was asking me questions about their behaviour, it was clear she was watching them out the corner of her eye. Within half an hour, she had the measure of their personalities: the easygoing dolt (Janet), the she-Napoleon (Bootsy), the sunny survivor (Pablo), the troubled rock star (Ralph), the office joker (Shipley) and the oversensitive necromancer (The Bear).

There was also the sense that my cats were in a special presence and were cognisant of it: they seemed drawn to any area that Vicky was in, as if by some magic talisman. Vicky wasn't one of the more mystically inclined cat therapists that would read your cat's horoscope for you, but, in her own way, perhaps she was speaking to them without opening her mouth or looking in their direction, a feline form of the Stephen King concept of 'shining'. Their typical characteristics seemed heightened, though clearly this in itself was very exhausting work for them, since, from what I can work out, each of them slipped into a mild coma for about fifteen hours straight afterwards.

The morning after Vicky left, I arrived in the living room to find Ralph and Pablo both sitting within five feet of one another on the floor, in the paws-tucked-under pose known among cat owners variously as 'The Packed Chicken', 'The Duck', 'The Tea Cosy' and 'Monorail Cat'.

I called Dee over. 'Have you seen this?'

'Wow! Unheard of,' she exclaimed. 'And they're doing The Tea Cosy.'

It might have seemed a small point to an outsider, but The Tea Cosy was strictly the jurisdiction of The Bear and Shipley. It simply wasn't Pablo and Ralph's Thing. When they settled down, they were sprawlers and curlers and stretchers. When you were as used to their habits as we were, to see them in this uncharacteristic pose was no less odd than seeing a turtle sitting up at a writing desk.

My cats seemed to be experiencing the same phenomenon with Vicky that I'd experienced with every good teacher or coach I'd ever had: when your mentor's voice was still fresh in your head, you could carry out their instructions successfully, but once it began to fade, the problems began again. A week after her departure, the cats' Buddhist-like state of enlightenment had ebbed away, and the old fights had begun around the cat door again, but by that point a man called Jim from a company called Jim'll Fix It was on his way round to tunnel through the back wall of the top floor of the house and insert an exit and entrance point which would, I hoped, cure all Ralph's neuroses.

This was expensive, but could be looked upon positively as a final touch to a lengthy project – that last thing, to add to the room on the bottom floor that had essentially had all other uses suspended in order for it to act as a giant cat doormat, the special blankets on almost every chair in the house, the 'paw plank' bridging the gap between the conservatory roof and the balcony, and the fence built to stop the cats getting on the road – that made it not merely a house that was convenient for cats, but one that appeared to have been specifically designed for their capricious needs.

It didn't surprise or particularly worry me that Ralph didn't take to the new cat flap immediately. It led directly out onto the balcony: an area that, in summer, The Bear effectively used as his own penthouse flat: a place where he could enjoy his aging bachelordom away from those peers of his who weren't quite so appreciative of highbrow culture. Ralph wasn't scared of The Bear, but he knew to keep away, so it was perhaps only natural that I had to go out and gently encourage him over from the conservatory roof, then feed his well-upholstered flanks through the tunnel by hand. It was painstaking work, but I tried to believe that, if I did it enough times, Ralph would start to see it as normal. That said, the fact that the routine was still the same after three weeks was slightly worrying.

'It's a waiting game,' said Dee. 'You've got to prove you're the tougher one of the two of you.' How long, though, would I have to wait? For me, having held out and not let him in through a door for several weeks already felt a bit like I'd performed some gargantuan emotional fasting ritual. I tried sitting it out completely, lying in bed while Ralph sat outside the bedroom window, telling me that he was 'Raaalph!' An hour would go by, and there'd be breaks in the Raaalphing, but it would always start up again. Since Ralph apparently had no other pressing business awaiting him, there was clearly only going to be one winner here.

The moment I finally cracked was during a morning about four weeks after Vicky's visit, when I'd gone out to the balcony to encourage Ralph over from the conservatory roof – the usual final part of our morning ritual, which began with me calling 'Ralphy!' down to him, and, upon seeing me, him changing his 'Raaalph!' to a slightly pathetic, high-pitched squeak in my direction.

'He makes that noise because he thinks you're his mum,' Dee would tell me. 'He'd probably like to suckle you as well, if he got the chance.' Ralph had actually started using the new cat flap by this point, but only after I'd coaxed him over from the roof and quickly bolted indoors, often watched from indoors by Pablo who, with his tongue protruding, appeared to be giving the whole matter some serious thought.

Earlier that summer, Dee had draped some loose willow screening across the conservatory roof, in an attempt to help keep the morning sun out of the bedroom. This also provided a sound buffer, lessening the thump when the cats landed on the roof. Most of them used the paw plank to pass from the roof to the balcony but Ralph had always seemed suspicious of it, and preferred to leap the four-foot gap. Now, with one more encouraging 'Ralphy!' I watched as he launched himself from on top of the willow screening. I then continued to watch as the willow screening came loose beneath him, serving to flip him up almost vertically, with no forward propulsion, as if a table cloth had been inexpertly pulled from beneath him, and he toppled, legs splaying, to the ground below.

The fall was no more than nine or ten feet, and I could see that Ralph was unhurt, but, grabbing the nearest available footwear, without looking what it was, and forcing my feet into it, I raced downstairs and outside to find him. He had that 'stolen mittens' look again, and was sitting behind a phormium, licking his lips nervously. If I looked at the incident objectively, he had caused the hardship to himself, right from his first cold-blooded attacks on Pablo to the misjudged idiocy of his jump, but that would be overlooking the fact that I am fundamentally unable to view any incident involving my cats objectively. I hadn't felt this guilty

since the time I'd thrown an empty cardboard box in his
direction in exasperation after he'd maimed a pregnant rat.

I knew now that my resolve would crumble, and, tomorrow morning – maybe even this afternoon – I'd open the
door for him when he asked me to. That wasn't such a terrible thing to do, was it? I'd spent most of my childhood in
houses with two cats and no cat flap. Other people had
alarm clocks; I didn't need to waste money on one, as I had
cats. And, besides, wasn't the morning the best part of the
day: for working, for taking in the air, for *being alive*? Those
people who could sleep through the noise their cats made –
they were the ones missing out.

I sat on the wall next to the patio, looked down towards
the lake at the end of the garden, and listened to the sounds
of a small British country town at 6.30 am: the flap of a
crow's wings, the odd quack, the distant rumble of a train on
the Norwich to London line. Ralph, his dignity now
regained, trotted over to me, rubbed his lip against my
finger, and made that high-pitched meow again. Sure, you
could call it 'girly', but he was a cat, and surely the feline
playing field was one where traditional notions of girliness
could be disregarded? As for this 'mum' business, I didn't see
any evidence of that here. We were just two blokes, taking
in the air. Shortly, we would both go off to do our blokey
things. Ralph would retire to plan his next battle strategy,
eat some meat, like men do, and fall asleep in any sprawling
way he wanted, not caring who judged him for it. I would
clear up the beer cans that last night's arguers had thrown
over the fence, then go inside, take Dee's glittery pumps off
my feet, and set about the business of earning a living. But
before that, we would just take a minute more, together, to
enjoy the brief, unusual silence.

Animals I Have Considered Stealing. Number One: The People Sheep

NAME:
The People Sheep

OCCUPATION:
Sheep

HOME:
Banham Zoo, Norfolk, UK

BRIEF CV:
When you think of the word 'sheep', what you don't normally think of are phrases such as 'born raconteur', 'erudite zest for life' and 'Alain de Botton'. But The People Sheep is like no other sheep before him – not even that weird one that Gene Wilder takes to bed with him in *Everything You Always Wanted to Know About Sex but Were Too Afraid to*

Ask. He lives at the zoo about six miles from my house, in an enclosure between a pen housing some uniquely spoilt pygmy goats and a pot-bellied pig that, from what I can work out from my research, has been asleep in exactly the same position since June 2003.

In contrast to these neighbours, with their world-owes-us-a-living demeanours, The People Sheep stares out at his visitors with eager, bright intelligence, his hooves up on the fence as they pass. But do they pay attention? Do they feel the electric rays of his good nature? No, of course they don't. They are too busy looking forward to visiting some meerkats, about forty yards away.

I put to those visitors this question: What's so great about meerkats? What do they really give the world, apart from the art of sitting on their hind legs, looking sour, as if having smelled a distant, foul odour that they pretend offends them, but they secretly quite like? If that's the kind of thing that floats your boat, you don't need to go all the way to a zoo – you can just stay in and watch reruns of Fiona Phillips presenting *GMTV*. Does a meerkat radiate such professorial wit and charm that, when you leave him, you are convinced that he was wearing glasses, chewing on a pipe, and quoting from the early casuals of S.J. Perelman? No. I realise that one way of looking at it is 'Who wants to see a sheep in a zoo?' But I prefer to take a different standpoint: the standpoint of, 'If a sheep has made it into a zoo, that sheep must be a unique specimen – a veritable hero among sheep.'

PROS:
Great dinner parties. Effortlessly neat lawn. Winning, show-boating comeback for those frequent 'But sheep don't actually really do anything, do they?' debates.

CONS:
I actually quite like mowing the lawn.

The Man Who Cried Chaffinch

'AH SAY, JO, HAVE YOU SEEN THIS? AH SAY, JO, HAVE YOU SEEN THIS? TOM, AH SAY, SWITCH THAT FOOKING BOLLOCKS OFF AND COME AND SEE THIS.'

It was 1994, and I was upstairs in my bedroom in my mum and dad's country cottage listening to the first Smashing Pumpkins album, and wondering why I could never quite get my hair the way Jim Morrison's looked in the poster on my wall. My mum was downstairs, making a mouse out of felt. My dad was standing by the kitchen window, and he was excited. My dad is almost always excited, so it would perhaps be most accurate to say he was even more excited than normal. A sure sign that he was more excited than normal was that he had used the expression 'AH SAY'.

My dad had been using the expression 'AH SAY' for as long as I could remember. And, for very nearly as long as I could remember, my mum and I had been trying, unsuccessfully, to wean him off doing so. As in the case of a select group of other northern and almost-northern men born around the middle of the twentieth century, 'AH SAY', for my dad, was a more rough and ready, nagging version of the posher, better known phrase 'I say!' If he was using it, it meant he wanted your attention, and he wanted it that instant. You could attempt to ignore him, carry on making your ingenious felt rodent or playing with your hair in the hope it would finally stop sitting on your head like a straw mushroom, but you'd be wasting your time, since, in the end, you'd be required to succumb to a greater force.

On the scale of parent–adolescent irritation, hearing my dad shout 'AH SAY!' was right up there with him waking me up by playing avant-garde jazz albums at 6.30 in the morning, and I'm sure, right now, I would have reminded him of this fact, had I not looked out the window towards our lawn and seen a weasel ripping a rabbit's throat out.

'HAVE YOU SEEN IT?' said my dad. 'FOOKING INCREDIBLE.'

'Oh god, that's awful,' my mum and I chimed.

'SHHHHHHH,' said my dad, who seemed unaware that, for the last five minutes, he was, with the exception of the Smashing Pumpkins, the only person in the house who'd been making any noise of note. 'IF YOU'RE QUIET YOU CAN HEAR IT.'

Sure enough, through the glass, I could hear *something*. You might not have presumed it was the sound of an animal at first. Not that it was the noise of a machine, exactly, more that some deep, dark, rasping part of the rabbit had chosen to speak for itself, bypassing the mouth and vocal cords. As for what it was trying to say, it couldn't be put into words: it was too primal, too visceral and remote.

'Can't we do something about it?' said my mum. 'It's screaming for its life.'

'I'm going to go outside and clap my hands, then maybe it will be able to escape,' I said.

'NO,' said my dad. 'YOU'VE GOT TO LET NATURE TAKE ITS COURSE. ANYWAY, LOOK: IT'S GOT HALF ITS THROAT HANGING OUT NOW.'

On further reflection, it was indeed clear that little could have been done for the rabbit. We watched as the weasel dragged it across the lawn and into the hedge, then turned back to our business, each of us – even my dad – shocked into silence. A few hours later, as dusk was falling, I crept out onto the dew-soaked lawn in my slippers and peered into the spot in the hedgerow where the weasel and its prey had disappeared, but saw nothing. I was still upset, but an 'out of hedge, out of mind' rule came into play. If there was no slaughtered rabbit in my garden, then I still lived in a world consisting not of slaughtered rabbits but of the faultless tousle of Jim Morrison's hair circa 1967 and that perfect, electrifying moment on track two of the Smashing Pumpkins' *Gish* album when the thundering guitar shoots from the left speaker, to the right speaker, and then back again.

I'd been hearing the nocturnal noises coming through my open bedroom window from the field, or, terrifyingly, even closer, for a few months now: the guttural cries of unidentified creatures. Some tiny, or – going on this latest evidence – perhaps not so tiny, squeaky, furry thing meeting a horrifically elongated end. When humans were being murdered, they screamed, but that was understandable. To find that animals did too was far more bewildering. Did the vole skewered by the talons of the tawny owl think that if it raised its voice loud enough, a tiny vole army would appear at the top of the hill, blowing their tiny vole horns, form a vole pyramid and pull their brother from the owl's clutches and safely back to earth? And who precisely did the rabbit think was coming to its rescue? Come to think of it, I preferred not to dwell on that one.

My parents and I had moved into our rented cottage, a couple of miles from the northeast Midlands village of Ockwold, three months earlier, relocating from a housing estate in the Nottingham suburbs. To me, the place was a giant, uncool inconvenience: something that put me that bit further away from any dingy, sticky venue playing the dingy, sticky indie rock that had become my fleeting obsession. To my mum, it was a tranquil contrast to her job in an urban primary school: somewhere where she could listen to the uninterrupted dawn chorus and make magical items out of fabric. To my dad, it was the realisation of a lifelong dream. We'd lived in the countryside before, but this was the real deal – a truly isolated spot, ringed for miles by deep woodland.

Besides the two cottages next door and the farms a couple of hundred yards on either side of us, you would have had to walk a mile in order even to see another building. Living in a temporary, all-consuming fog of discordant guitar, blinding me to the beauty of anything else, I planned to leave the place as soon as humanly possible; a plan I felt the need to put into practice even more quickly when, only two days after we moved in, the local gamekeeper brought us a special housewarming present.

'Is that a . . . hare?' I asked my dad as he closed the door on his new friend.

'YEAH. IT'S BLOODY AMAZING, ISN'T IT?'

'It's bloody terrible, that's what it is. How can he do that?'

My dad held the hare – not gingerly, yet not quite confidently either. For all his wide-eyed excitement, he probably didn't know quite what was next. Was he supposed to skin it? Take it straight to a cooking pot? Hang it up on the front door to ward off evil? He'd been brought culinary offerings by neighbours in the past, of course, but the home-made Bombay mix given to us by the Indian couple next door to our last house didn't quite throw up the same set of dilemmas.

The two of us stood frozen in the hare's eyes in much the same way the animal itself might once have frozen in the headlights of one of the cars that rocketed antisocially along the adjacent lane. Then the unthinkable happened: as we stared, one of them began to move, revealing a bluebottle, which, having wriggled out of the corner of the socket, crawled along the sleeve of my dad's cardigan.

Later that night, I relayed this information to my girlfriend, Jenny, and we agreed that we had reached the last straw: what with this, and what Morrissey had said on The Smiths' *Meat Is Murder* LP, how could we any longer go on living with ourselves, without being vegetarians?

I'd been spellbound by the folksy magic of hares – rock star rabbits, unshackled by the 'straight' mammal world – right from when I'd pawed repeatedly through the pages of Kit Williams' *Masquerade* as a seven-year-old. At anything but this most pretentious stage of my life, my sadness at seeing one dead would undoubtedly have been offset by my fascination at seeing one close up at all. At eighteen, the idea of having a wild animal killed by a human and brought into the place where I lived did not just offend my belief that all creatures should be treated with kindness, it offended my belief that all life worth living happened in the city, and involved people between the ages of seventeen and twenty-five.

My dad looked at the hare from an entirely different standpoint: I'm sure he didn't endorse the idea of killing it, but I'm equally sure that his excitement of being confronted with such raw, pulsating rural life drowned out his misgivings.

My dad had always been liable to frenzied outbursts on seeing animals. 'FOOKTIVANO! LOOK AT THAT! SODDING SPECTACULAR!' he would often shout, on a drive in Derbyshire, braking sharply upon seeing a giant bull in a nearby field, as, mindful of previous mishaps, my mum would make a dive for the steering wheel. In our new home, however, every day seemed to bring a new animal-themed exclamation.

'GOOLIES! OH MY FOOKIN' GOD!' I would hear him shout. From the patriarch of any other family, this might have meant that a digit had been severed or a close relative had been found collapsed on the kitchen floor in a pool of their own making, but my mum and I knew it probably just meant that the bloodhounds from the local hunt were coming over the hill across the lane or the gamekeeper had brought him some more pheasants.

At this point, my dad was still working as a supply teacher – a job he'd been doing on and off for over a decade. On the days when a school didn't call upon his services, he could mostly be found in his study, painting a bull he'd photographed on his travels or one of the horses in the field at the rear of the house, or my cat, Monty. Every so often, if I happened to be in the house, working on an essay or my self-published music magazine, he would shout to ask me if

I could make him some coffee. I would go downstairs and do so, then place the mug by his side, where it would be left to go cold, just like the eight previous mugs surrounding it. 'LOOK AT THAT,' he might then say, pointing out the window.

'What?' I would reply, peering into the sky, and spotting nothing of interest.

'BLOODY SPARROWHAWK, YOU TWAZZOCK, ISN'T IT?'

I'm sure that, for many strangers, coming into our house and hearing my dad swear at me might have seemed odd, but I knew that the vast majority of his profanities were not attacks upon my character. For the two of us, phrases such as 'twazzock', 'fookpig' and 'shit basket' served in much the same way as 'pal', 'mate' and 'son' served in other father–son relationships. He'd always cursed a lot, and the moment a few years earlier when he'd finally started directing his cursing at me had made me feel grown-up and proud: a bit like an atheist's version of a bar mitzvah.

'Oh, right,' I said.

'WHAT DO YOU MEAN, "OH RIGHT"?'

'Well, the way I see it, it's just a bird, and there are lots of birds around here. You get used to them after a while, and they all kind of look the same.'

'"ALL LOOK THE SAME!?" ALL LOOK THE SAME!? DO YOU HAVE ANY SODDING IDEA WHAT YOU'RE SAYING? YOU DON'T KNOW YOU'RE BORN. FOOK-ING UNBELIEVABLE, YOU TOSSPOT. I CAN'T BELIEVE YOU. *JO-O-O! COME UPSTAIRS AND LISTEN TO WHAT TOM'S JUST SAID! YOU WON'T BELIEVE IT!*'

In theory, our new home was the quietest place we had

ever lived, but, with my dad around, in his hyped-up state, it soon became the noisiest. Who knows? I suppose he could have thrown himself into rural life more rambunctiously: he didn't learn to ride a horse or take up the open invitation from our middle-aged loner of a next-door neighbour, Frank, to 'come fox shooting'. But he made a pretty good job of insinuating himself into local life and, before long, local animals, perhaps sensing a fellow force of nature, began to gravitate towards him.

Of the two farms nearby, just one actually functioned as a farm. This was owned by a grumpy man called Warren, whose grimy agricultural face, it was claimed by some in the area, would fall off if he ever cracked a smile. The other farm served as a babysitting business for racehorses – or, as my mum described it, a 'horse cattery' – run by our third closest neighbours, the Pattens. That summer, when one of these horses escaped onto the narrow lane, my dad was first on the scene, blocking its path in one direction with his Ford Mondeo estate, stopping another passing driver and inveigling him to do the same, then racing down to the farmhouse to tell the Pattens that one of their charges had escaped, though not before poking his head in through our front door to shout, 'TOM, COME AND HAVE A SOD-DING LOOK AT THIS. NOW! COME NOW!'

My dad's good deed led to an arrangement enabling him to take a wheelbarrow up to the Pattens' place whenever he needed manure. He seemed unfathomably enthusiastic about this, with the exception of the day when the Pattens had been out and he returned to the house looking some-what outraged, having had his shovelling session interrupted by two irate Irishmen wielding an out-of-control stallion.

'ORDERING ME AROUND THEY WERE,' my dad said, returning to the house in his slip-on shoes, oversized polo shirt and baggy cords, stained with manure and last night's mayonnaise. 'COUPLE OF FOOKPIGS! KEPT TELLING ME TO OPEN UP THE GATES AND ASKING ME WHERE TO PUT THE BLOOMIN' GREAT THING. I WAS BUGGERED IF I WOULD BE GOING NEAR IT. I COULD SEE IT WANTED TO GO FOR ME. IT WOULD HAVE KICKED MY FACE OFF. DO I LOOK LIKE A SODDING STABLE BOY?'

Another day, not long after that, he returned from answering the door to tell my mum and me that he'd just been asked to shoot a deer.

'What, just for fun?' I asked. Having lived in this environment for a year now, such a leisure pursuit would hardly have surprised me.

'NO, YOU STUPID STREAK OF PISS, HE'D RUN IT OVER AND WANTED ME TO PUT IT OUT OF ITS MISERY. IT'S IN THE BACK SEAT OF HIS CAR. I TOLD HIM TO GO AND SEE WARREN AT THE FARM.'

Twenty minutes later, the three of us were jolted up from the night's curry by a loud bang.

'FOOKTIVANO,' said my dad. 'I SUPPOSE THAT MEANS THAT WARREN JUST SHOT IT. EITHER THAT OR HE JUST GOT REALLY PISSED OFF THAT THE BLOKE HAD DISTURBED HIS TEA AND DECIDED TO TAKE REVENGE.'

At the bottom of the garden, my mum and dad had transformed one of our sheds into a run for eight Pekin bantam chickens: Egbert, Punk, Panic, Pandemonium, Henrietta, Egatha, Snowshoes and Moonboots. I briefly got involved in their upkeep, teaching them to jump on my knee and take scraps from my hand. When Henrietta arrived in the kitchen in a large amount of discomfort having half-laid an egg, my mum and I were on hand to perform a DIY rescue operation involving a bowl of warm water and some rubber gloves. This proved successful, although, following careful consideration, I chose not to boast about it to my friends at Nottingham Rock City's weekly Alternative Night the following evening.

But, by and large, when an animal-related incident happened to the Cox family, my dad was the one it happened to. On one hand, there was a very obvious reason for this: my dad lived in a constant state of high alert, and was always the first to answer our phone or door. But I also sometimes got the sense that animals saw my dad as separate from other, less instinctual humans; a rival, almost. When my mum was cooking meat, it was not uncommon to see Monty and him congregating around her. Certainly, their methods were different – Monty was a clever cat but had not worked out to communicate his hunger to my mum by saying, 'AH SAY, JO, WHEN WILL IT BE READY, AH SAY?' so instead settled for a gaze deep into her eyes and a gentle claw in the calf muscle – but the intention was the same. Egbert, our rooster, remained largely indifferent to me, yet, when my dad appeared in the garden, would hurl himself at his legs the second his back was turned.

'HE'S AFTER ME AGAIN, JO,' my dad would complain to my mum. 'FOOKIN' FOOKPIG. CAN YOU BELIEVE IT? WHY DOES HE NEVER GO FOR TOM?'

'He must think your dad's after his birds,' my mum confided to me. 'Or perhaps he just doesn't like all the noise. He's a very quiet rooster, really.'

I was definitely not complaining about being exempt from the action. If I could get through the day without witnessing the death or maiming of an animal, that would mean I would also get through the day without having to make conversation with one of the neighbours. On the evenings when my parents were out, I'd live in constant dread that a knock at the door would reveal another wounded deer. Jenny and I saw ourselves as animal lovers, but ours was a tame animal kingdom, consisting of cats and dogs and gerbils, and, alone in the house, listening to our Smiths LPs, that was the way we intended to keep it. So when Jenny went downstairs to get a choc ice, and I heard her yelp, I feared the worst.

'What is it? Are you okay?' I shouted.

'There's a . . . something in the freezer. It was horrible. I literally don't have *any idea* what it is.'

I'd known friends to have extreme reactions to my mum's more exotic cooking before – one golfing pal who'd come over for dinner had been rather perturbed to see his first aubergine – but Jenny was a fairly worldly girl, and I couldn't believe that she'd be that taken aback by a frozen moussaka.

'It's a . . . thing,' she said, pointing me towards the freezer. 'I don't think it should be in there. I don't think it's hygienic.'

What was perhaps strangest of all is that when I followed her into the pantry, and found myself staring at a sealed plastic bag containing the long-eared bat that Monty had slaughtered and abandoned on the kitchen floor the previous week, it didn't even come as that much of a shock. Even a moment later, when I discovered a grasshopper warbler behind a bag of value price sweetcorn, I amazed myself with my aura of serenity. I did, however, make a quick mental note: when entertaining friends in future, I'd make sure that I was the one to fetch the snacks.

'I'M THINKING OF HAVING THEM STUFFED,' my dad explained, upon arriving home, later that night. 'THEY'RE BLOODY RARE. I FEEL BAD THAT MONTY KILLED THEM. I FEEL LIKE DOING SOMETHING TO MAKE UP FOR IT. YOU CAN'T JUST SHOVE STUFF LIKE THAT IN THE BIN OR IN A HEDGE, CAN YOU?'

There is a certain type of man to be found in provincial Britain who will keep a dead badger in his freezer with no real concern for what society might think of him. Elsewhere in his house, you will find sinks lined with a thick film of old hair and window ledges dotted with an inexplicable quantity of empty milk cartons. I hasten to point out that my dad is not this man. On the other hand, by his mid-forties, he'd had enough experience with taxidermy for stuffed animals to be slightly normalised for him.

Around a decade earlier, between supply teaching jobs, he had accepted a nebulous part-time position as Artist in Residence at an educational resource centre just outside Nottingham. Farnley House was a large Georgian building set high on a hill in deep forestry commission land. Inside, it resembled the lair of some Victorian eccentric shut-in philanthropist, and played host to a selection of equally eccentric refugees from the school staffrooms of the East

Midlands. These included Rod, a Samurai sword-obsessed former English teacher who was continually having motor-bike accidents, a roll-up-smoking taxidermist called Ben, and an eagle-beaked man with flowing blond locks and leather trousers known sometimes as Mike but mostly just as 'Zeppelin' who had a terrifying habit of pinching people's legs just above their knees when they weren't expecting it.

As the only child of two teachers, I was accustomed to finding ways to amuse myself in big, semi-deserted 200-year-old buildings. Having quickly exhausted the infotainment potential of Mr Chester's Big Trak and Miss Davies' budgerigars at Claremont, the primary school where I studied and my mum taught English as a Second Language, I'd learned to use my imagination to get myself through the hour between the school bell and my mum's home-time. But, wandering the corridors at Farnley, there was always something new to be discovered – a hitherto unknown chamber containing a selection of dusty marsupials or the cobwebbed paraphernalia of a 1930s shop window. Kept in walnut boxes, these items were borrowed only once in a blue moon.

As I wandered the corridors of Farnley, I usually avoided Ben The Taxidermist's room, though I would occasionally peek through the open doorway. The smell of viscera and formaldehyde was overpowering, and I was scared of Ben's eagle owl, Fred, who would sit on Ben's shoulder as he worked, gazing down sternly yet approvingly as Ben hollowed out the thorax of a stoat or squirrel. When I'd first been introduced to him, Ben had placed Fred briefly on my shoulder, but I'd sensed Fred wasn't strictly up for it, and my dad had actually had to hold my shoulder in place, what with Fred being the size of my entire nine-year-old torso.

Fred went everywhere with Ben, including, occasionally, to some of my dad's supply teaching jobs, where Ben would occasionally give talks to children about his work with animals. After half a decade, my dad had learned that supply teaching was a bite-or-be-bitten world, and the stuffed beasts he brought to his classes from Farnley proved an invaluable distraction: by being Stuffed Animal Guy, he could avoid being Persecuted Supply Teacher Guy. Most of my dad's regular schools got used to seeing an inanimate fox or baby capybara in the corner of their staffroom, though the Deputy Headmistress of one was perturbed to notice the large, dead owl on the table next to her, only for Fred to very slowly swivel his head in her direction and offer her a single, ominous blink.

My dad once reported that Ben's mum had cleaned out the freezer and found his childhood guinea pig, Tootles – who had, it should be added, died of natural causes – and Ben, who'd forgotten all about him, had cried for a whole afternoon.

'When Fred dies, will Ben stuff him?' I asked my dad.

'PROBABLY. IT WILL BE KIND OF A TRIBUTE.'

'But he won't stuff him before he's dead, will he?'

'NO. OF COURSE NOT.'

'But if he likes animals so much, why does he like it when they're dead?'

'I'M NOT SURE. ASK YOUR MUM. NOW, I'VE GOT TO FINISH PAINTING THIS GOAT, SO CAN WE TALK ABOUT IT LATER?'

Despite what my dad had assured me, it did turn out that Ben's interest in taxidermy wasn't *strictly* limited to dead creatures. I found this out one day upon coming home from school and discovering my dad crouched in front of the living room coffee table, upon which sat a hard white blob about the size of a builder's fist.

'AH SAY, TOM, COME 'ERE AND SEE THIS,' said my dad.

'What is it?' I said.

'SSSSHHHHH!' said my dad. 'YOU'VE GOT TO BE REALLY QUIET OR YOU'LL WAKE HIM.'

I could now see that the white blob had legs and eye-holes. 'Is that a toad?' I asked.

'YES. HE'S GOT HIS PROTECTIVE WINTER COAT-ING ON. PICK HIM UP IF YOU LIKE, BUT BE VERY CAREFUL BECAUSE IF HE GETS DISTURBED HE WILL GET ANGRY AND BREAK OUT OF IT. LIKE THE INCREDIBLE HULK DOES. THEN HE WILL PROBABLY BITE YOU.'

After I had picked up the white blob and ascertained that it contained only air, not amphibian, the full story emerged. That morning, a bored Ben had ventured out into the woods behind Farnley House and chloroformed a toad and taken it back to his workroom. He'd then covered it in dental putty, being careful to leave a breathing hole, and allowed the putty to set for the next few hours. At the end of the day, he'd been back to the woods, cut the dried putty, and released the toad, who'd staggered off into the woods like the drugged hostage of unexpectedly kindly terrorists. The casing had then been resealed and loaned to my dad for the evening.

If Malcolm, the frequently sozzled, sexagenarian art collector whose job it was to oversee Farnley, was aware of his workforce's antics, he did not show it. Nobody ever got to the bottom of who it was that ham-fistedly altered the sign at the bottom of the drive which said 'Farnley House:

Educational Resource Centre' to make it say 'Ed's Occasional Racehorse Centre' but it was a full month before anybody was concerned enough to change it back.

In the foyer of Farnley hung a giant painting of a nude youth by the artist Albert Wainwright. For ten days in a row, my dad painstakingly painted and cut out a different theme of underwear, including thongs, Speedos and some masterfully designed Hawaiian boxer shorts, and stuck it over the youth's crotch area. When Malcolm arrived in the morning, my dad and Zeppelin would hide out on the balcony above and watch his reaction, which normally involved staring quizzically at the picture for around thirty seconds, as if trying to work out exactly what was different about it, then moving on. Neither did Malcolm ever seem quite aware of the litter of baby hedgehogs brought in by Ben, which often made short work of the cheese sandwich leftovers in Farnley's staffroom.

Eventually, my dad's role was expanded at Farnley to include overseeing many of the educational items that were sent out to schools. Every so often, he'd receive a call asking for an authentic eighteenth-century musket or a duck-billed platypus, but on the whole the pace remained sluggish.

By this point, our house had become a temporary home for many of the animals that my dad did not feel were getting the respect they deserved at Farnley. Strangely, it has taken me over two decades to realise there's anything remotely odd about having a polar bear guarding your entrance hall, and with this realisation comes the inevitable cavalcade of other questions. How exactly did my dad fit it into the boot of a Morris Marina? When Paul Abbott's mum phoned up my mum to say he couldn't stay over at my house any more, was it really just because Paul was 'having trouble sleeping without the light on in a foreign house' or was there more to it than that? When Paul closed his eyes, was he experiencing a generic fear of the dark, or was he specifically thinking about the giant claws and enormous, toothy muzzle just a few feet below him?

The polar bear was actually a little too demented-looking, a bit wonky around the chops, to genuinely strike fear into the heart of most visitors. More black-fanged and impressive was the baby alligator that slept at the end of my bed throughout the summer of 1985, and briefly made me the most popular boy in my school year. After Darren Kestembaum stayed over and I placed it on his chest facing him while he was asleep, a rumour developed in Mr Highland's class that I actually owned a real alligator. While I never went so far as to confirm this, neither did I quite discourage it.

Sadly, by the time most of the class began to invite themselves over, the alligator had gone to stay with Zeppelin, and, subsequently, his grandma, who was reportedly using it as a draught excluder. However, I think my new friends found some consolation for its absence in my dad interrupting our rice pudding to bring in a stuffed ocelot and announce, 'THIS IS TIBBLES: I GOT HIM FROM THE RSPCA RECENTLY. HE'S GOT A BIT OF A BAD TEMPER BUT HE'S OKAY ONCE YOU GET TO KNOW HIM.'

When Farnley closed, the collection moved to smaller premises, and many of its animals came up for grabs. In the end, after careful consideration, the polar bear chose to co-habit with Farnley's janitor, a bachelor called Eric who lived in a one-bedroom flat near Nottingham city centre and, it must be assumed, was not subject to a large amount of lady callers. The ocelot went to Zeppelin, who had already taken to keeping it on the back shelf of his Mark 1 Ford Capri, often accompanied by a marmot, putting him a level up from fellow East Midlands playboys who settled for fluffy dice and a pine-scented air freshener.

The tawny owl, fox and African mole rat my dad brought home all put in their time as domestic sentries, educational devices and practical-joke props over the next few years, but history does not record where their afterlife journeys came to an end, or if they still continue, elsewhere, against the odds. Had I not turned into an adolescent, and temporarily lost my fascination with the natural world, I probably would have paid more attention.

'Oh, that old thing?' my mum will say now, as I ask her about the mole rat. 'I don't know. One of its legs fell off in the end, though. I remember that much. I think I took it to the antiques fair with me one time and my friend Sandra bought it off me. Or no, maybe that was the fox.'

In the end, the sole Farnley refugee to survive my teenage years was not a wild animal at all, but a West Highland terrier. I'd named it Rags, after the electronic dog in the Woody Allen film *Sleeper*, which, as an eleven-year-old, I'd adored. Our Rags had none of the perky, waggy-tailed charm of its namesake, and his off-white fur was less than strokable, but every summer he would sit in our front window, sometimes for up to four weeks, obediently guarding our home while we were on our annual holiday. To my knowledge, nobody called the RSPCA on us, though we did return from Italy in 1988 to find our neighbours, Dennis and Roma, standing at our front gate looking pale and worried. Having already had to report the death of my goldfish that summer, which had long ago gone to live in their pond, my heart bleeds to think of the emotional steeling they must have done before giving us the tragic news that our pet dog had 'not moved' for an entire fortnight.

Rags survived several house moves in the late 80s and early 90s, and made it to the cottage near Ockwold. It was in our third summer here that, undaunted by age and the physical effects of frequently getting the crud beaten out of him by Monty, he embarked on his most heroic and selfless adventure yet.

There wasn't a lot of traffic on the narrow lane outside the cottage, but what there was would not be out of place in a wacky, computer-based racing game: a mixture of horses, stock cars heading to the racetrack two miles away, tractors, combine harvesters, stolen Ford Escorts and police cars. Not all of these sights raised a smile, but one that did was the weekly trundle of a mobility scooter, driven by an obese disabled lady, upon whose roof travelled a proud-looking Jack Russell.

I have no idea where the lady in the mobility scooter lived, nor where she travelled to every Tuesday, but she seemed very determined about it. She always rode along in the centre of the lane, her bespectacled face a mask of belligerence, and she and her Jack Russell appeared unfazed on the occasions when a farm vehicle or local boy-racer was being held up behind her. Sometimes, up to four vehicles could be seen queuing up in her slipstream. My bedroom and my dad's workroom faced the lane, and we would often stop work to watch these processions, although on the occasion she had her accident we were on the other side of the house in the garden.

'FOOKTIVANO! WAS THAT YOU?' my dad asked me, switching off his hedge clippers.

'Was what me?' I said.

'THAT FOOKIN MASSIVE SQUAWKING NOISE YOU MADE. LIKE ONE OF THE MONTY PYTHON WOMEN.'

'I haven't done that for years.'

'Ceaaaaaakkkwwww!'

'THERE IT WAS AGAIN. SEE WHAT I MEAN? JUST LIKE THE WOMAN IN THE SPAM SKETCH.'

'Yeah. But it wasn't me. Did you see my lips move?'

My dad and I hurried down the garden, in the direction of the cawing sound, through the gate and into the downhill track leading to the Pattens' farmhouse.

Simultaneously, we spotted the wheel sticking up out of the ditch, twenty yards down the track. The scooter was wedged fast, and its occupant was wedged even faster inside the scooter, still making the cawing sound. Perhaps, initially, the noise had been more like 'Heeelp!' but, as she'd spent longer there, and hope of human assistance had dimmed, it had degenerated into something more desperate, a last-ditch appeal from a ditch to any benevolent crows who happened to be passing.

Getting the scooter back upright, with its driver – whom it now emerged was called Beryl – still inside it, meant my dad and I getting into the ditch and heaving, red-faced, with all our strength. A grunt or two could have helped, but both of us remained near silent as we pushed, aware of how such a noise might, in the circumstances, seem tactless, given Beryl's physique. I was enormously relieved to see the scooter back upright – not just because Beryl was unhurt, but because we'd managed our rescue operation without me having to resort to my dad's original suggestion of getting help from Frank, the fox-hater next door, who disturbed me, and probably would have brought his gun, just on the off chance that there was something with a snout involved that needed putting out of its misery.

'Ceaaaaaakkkwwww! I don't know what happened,' said Beryl. 'I was pootling along, and I just lost control, and it ran away from me down the hill.'

As we ascertained that the scooter was still working, my dad asked her if she needed any help getting home.

'No, no, I'll be fine, ceaaaaaakkkwwww!' said Beryl, whose return to vertical life strangely did not seem to have diminished her enthusiasm for making crow-like Monty Python woman noises.

'I SEE YOU DRIVING DOWN HERE A LOT,' said my dad. 'WITH YOUR DOG, UP THERE ON THE ROOF. HE LOOKS LIKE HE ENJOYS IT.'

'Oh yes, my Billy. He's up there now.' Beryl pointed to the top of the mobility vehicle.

My dad and I exchanged a nervous glance, and scanned the roof, which was incontrovertibly dog-free.

'OOH, ER . . . RIGHT. ARE YOU SURE?' my dad asked Beryl.

I felt my heart sink somewhere south of my shins. We had been far too smug and hasty. How could we not have remembered the Jack Russell during our rescue operation? Had he been flipped over the hedge into the field? Was his inert form still lying in the ditch, half crushed? Perhaps I would need to get Frank and his gun after all.

'Yes, that's right,' said Beryl. 'Up there, in heaven. He'll be happy now. I had him put to sleep last week, poor little chap.'

Naturally, neither of us wanted to be seen as treating the death of Billy as good news, but I'm sure our relief must have been palpable, as it drained into our faces.

To further throw us off balance, Beryl added: 'You've still got your little fella, though, haven't you? I've seen him in your window. Lovely little frizzy white thing. Such a good boy, always on the lookout for you. Not like Billy. He never could sit still.'

My dad is no Jedi Master at thinking before he speaks, but in this instance he paused sensibly. I could see him asking himself the question: would it be helpful in any way to confront this woman, who recently lost what was quite possibly her only friend, who had barely finished wiping her tears away after the most traumatic of mornings, with more death and suffering?

'OH, YOU MEAN RAGS?' said my dad. 'HE'S FINE. THAT DOG JUST KEEPS GOING ON AND ON.'

For the next six months, Beryl continued to drive down the lane and, as she did, Rags was always sure to offer her his stoical greeting. Sometimes, for authenticity's sake, my dad or I would move him to a different window or add a cushion as a prop. One day Beryl drove by and I picked Rags up and made him wave to her. She didn't seem to suspect anything, but I sensed I was living a little close to the edge, thus refrained from a repeat performance. Rags' leg joint felt slightly brittle, and, as much as I liked playing practical jokes in my early twenties, I had no particular desire to put the fear of God into old ladies by waggling disembodied canine limbs at them.

By this point, one too many beatings from Monty's infamous back paws had taken their toll on Rags' coat, and his gums were beginning to come apart, revealing a congealed, sawdust-like substance. I considered taking him to be reupholstered, but, ultimately, what kind of person would that have made me? It was one thing being someone who owned a stuffed dog, but it was another thing entirely being someone who knew where to get that stuffed dog fixed up.

Rags made it through one more move, to my mum and dad's current house, on the Nottinghamshire–Lincolnshire border. The village of Kalterton is extremely rural, surrounded by water meadows and farms, but you're more likely to see a Range Rover on the nearby lane than a stolen car. My dad has never been asked to shoot anything by a neighbour or had to block in an escaped stallion with his car. The village did used to be home to a very sweet Shetland pony called Gladys who was permitted by her owners to wander around the lanes at will, but she was very well-mannered and, unlike a couple of the Shetlands once looked after by the Pattens, never wandered into anyone's kitchen uninvited and pilfered their cat food.

Monty died many years ago and the last family cat, Daisy, succumbed to cancer in 2007. The long-eared bat and grasshopper warbler were never stuffed in the end, hence did not survive the relocation. In 2004, my mum telephoned me to say that Egatha, her veteran bantam hen, had finally expired, following many false alarm 'sleep deaths'. This was sad, but also confusing, as I'd been under the impression Egatha had in fact died in 1997. 'Well, yes, she did,' admitted my mum. 'But I decided to change Snowshoes' name to Egatha towards the end. I think, on balance, she preferred it.'

As for Rags, I'd like to think that I was there to officially mark his departure, but the truth is I didn't actually notice he wasn't around any more until many weeks after he moved on. One day in 2007, after not giving him a thought for many parental visits, I simply turned round in the living room and suddenly sensed a fusty absence. I do think my mum was a little harsh taking him to the recycling centre with that week's garden waste, but I'm also forced to ask myself what I might have done in the same situation. Burial and cremation somehow wouldn't have quite seemed right, I doubt any museum or eBay buyer would have accepted him in his final, moth-eaten state, and as esoteric as many of my mum's friends are in their tastes for retro curios, I don't think any would have found a place for him on their stalls at the local antique market.

My parents and I have shared interests over the years, but very rarely have we shared them at the time. When they listened to Neil Young, I was busy playing golf. Now, at a time I would be rather pleased to have parents who listened to Neil Young, they give me a headache by playing loud French rap music and cacophonous African pop. Similarly, now it is too late, I would love little more than to return to a family home where Shetland ponies wandered in and ate the food of one of seven semi-feral cats, while an ocelot looked on superciliously from the top of the fridge. 'Why can't your mum and dad have a friend with an eagle owl when you want one?' I wonder, meditating on the cruel paradox that is my life.

My mum and dad do have some rather plump, colourful fish in the pond outside their back door. Their garden, they boast to me, has also recently been part-time home to a goldcrest, a yellowhammer, a redwing and several coal tits.

In the living room, in the summer, my mum holds a weekly life-drawing class, and opens up the French windows, enabling chaffinches and blue tits to add to the civilised late-middle-aged atmosphere by hopping about and feeding on a variety of overpriced seeds and nuts in the background. She tells of the time one of the models jerked up out of her lounging pose, and shouted, 'Bloomin' heck! Is that a puffin?' after spotting a greater spotted woodpecker on the birdfeeder.

'I don't know how she thought a puffin would have made its way to Kalterton!' my mum said.

It's a funny story, but when I heard it, my sympathies with the life model were stronger than I let on. I have nothing against birds, but to me they only become interesting when they get above a certain weight range. No doubt there will be a point in the future, probably when my parents have replaced their birdwatching with another hobby, when my latent ornithological gene will emerge, but until then, I view them as specks in the sky, preoccupied with their own thing. I have no desire to be up in their business, nor they to be down in mine.

'So isn't it time you got another pet?' I ask my mum now, frequently. She admits that she often considers it, but in the end, decides she quite likes living without the mess.

I suggest a dog.

'Oh, *no*. Too much hassle.'

'What about a goat?'

'Ooh, I don't think so. I think your dad and it might end up clashing.'

'Pigs can be very friendly.'

'But when would we ever get away?'

In the end, it's my suggestion of a new cat that's greeted

with the most enthusiasm, and we make tentative plans to go to a rescue centre, but she always changes her mind. ' I don't know. It just doesn't seem quite right just now. And I do like living in a clean house,' she says. My mum has somehow got the bizarre idea into her head that the small smattering of hair and occasional vomit deposited by a single feline constitutes 'dirt'.

She has seen the state of my carpet when I haven't vacuumed for three or four days, so it surprises me when she adds, 'I could maybe take one of yours off your hands if you want. At least I know that they're affectionate. It's different when you get one from the RSPCA.' I decline, and shake my head, amazed at how naive she is not to realise that this 'affection' she talks about is nothing genetic, merely the result of years of me catering to my cats' every whim, and that it might easily fade with the withholding of smoked salmon and the intimidating clatter of my dad's footsteps.

'WHAT'S THAT YOU'RE TALKING ABOUT?' says my dad, arriving in the kitchen. He's wearing chunky, baggy cords, has no top on, and is holding an electric tooth-flosser in one hand. In the other he holds a bag of mosquito larvae, which he has bought for his fish from the local Sunday market. Scrawled across his hands in Biro, I can see a list of the day's jobs, including 'MAKE PORRIDGE FOR BIRDS', 'CALL COUNCIL' and 'MANURE?'. He's about to offer his input to the pet conversation, but then he sees that two ducks have got into the pond. 'BLOOMIN' FOOKPIGS. MAKING THE WATER MUDDY AGAIN. I'LL BLOODY WRING THEIR NECKS!' he says, making his way quickly outside, dropping the tooth-flosser, which is still whirring, onto the kitchen table.

A couple of minutes later, I join him beside the pond. He's found an old shirt that he left in the garden yesterday and put it on, which pleases me. He's not wrung the ducks' necks, and never would, because deep down he loves them, but he has scared them off, and tranquillity has returned to the garden.

This tranquillity is broken almost immediately by the frantic whistle that my dad uses to tell the fish that it's mealtime. My ultimate feeling is that this whistle is plagiarism, a sped-up, inferior version of the one I use to get the attention of my cats, and that there isn't much point whistling at fish in the first place. Nonetheless, I let it go and do my best to look interested as he points out the Koi that's really fat, and eats nearly all the food, and the other Koi that's not quite as fat, but is still quite fat, and eats a lot of the food that the really fat one doesn't eat. He's lying flat on his stomach now, looking over the rim of the pond and studying the action, and I can tell he wants me to join him, just like I did when I was seven and we built a pond together and filled it with water beetles we'd collected from the lake up the road.

There's a commotion up above and my dad flips over onto his back. 'FOOKIN' HELL!' he shouts, looking up at the sky. 'LOOK AT THAT. BUZZARD! CAN YOU BELIEVE IT?'

I look up just in time to see a big black shape passing over the house. It's quite a startling sight, something I can properly get to grips with, not like the smaller shapes in the sky, which all blend into one, and I look for the right words to convey my surprise. 'That's . . . pretty impressive,' I say, and I mean it, but I know as soon as the words are out that they have a hollow, sarcastic ring to them, and I've got it very badly wrong. Even though I *am* genuinely impressed, I'm now back in a role that I've been playing so long, I don't know how to slip out of it.

My dad stands up and brushes the grass of his trousers. '"PRETTY IMPRESSIVE". IS THAT ALL YOU CAN SAY?' he says, heading back inside to finish flossing his teeth. 'YOU DON'T KNOW YOU'RE SODDING BORN.'

Excerpts from a Cat Owner's Diary

11 December 2007
Cat with extremely messed-up meow was meowing outside the back door today. Felt glad for not having cat with meow like that. Went outside. Was one of my cats, meowing like that.

1 March 2008
The Bear ate the last tin of his special Applaws cat food today. He *meeooped* all the way through it, as if to confirm just how mandatory it is that I reorder some of it at the earliest opportunity. I have known cats to meow for food before, but he is the first I've known to meow during it.

12 March 2008
When I see my cats smelling one another's noses, I can't help wondering: 'What exactly is it you think might have changed, since last time?'

4 September 2008
Lots of bands 'work on a new sound' late in their career. What is more surprising is when your cat starts doing the same thing.

14 September 2008
In her column in the *Mail On Sunday*'s *You* magazine, the infamously divorced, infamously childless, infamously cat-loving Liz Jones observes that her Old English sheepdog has begun to misbehave. 'He jumps at me all the time,' she complains, 'even when I am wearing my Dries van Noten jacket, which I have just had dry-cleaned.' This is an intriguing sentence on a couple of levels, but in the end it's the use of the word 'even' that really does it for me. One would have thought dogs would know a top designer jacket from normal daywear, but no. Cultural cretins! It's a bit bitchy to say it, but between you and me I wouldn't be surprised if that sheepdog hadn't even read the September issue of *Vogue*.

18 September 2008
I'm still not sure I can believe it myself, but I really did just use the term 'flailing paws' in a warning note to my cleaner.

19 September 2008
Signs that another market town summer is ending: 1) the air is suddenly fresh; 2) apples are falling; 3) The Bear is not wandering so far from home; 4) Summer Pablo is beginning to bulk up; 5) nobody kicked my car in last night.

13 October 2008
Two cats now 'working on new sound'. House starting to resemble Iggy Pop and David Bowie's 1970s Berlin, but with less clawing.

15 October 2008

I note with some interest that The Bear is now cultivating his own special 'piss meow'. I'm not necessarily looking on it as a bad thing, as it serves as more of a warning system than anything. I suppose it's a bit like a smoke alarm – except with piss, instead of smoke, obviously.

21 October 2008

Given the reputed commonness of the activity, it is surprising more celebrities don't reference their Daily Cat Puke Cleaning Session in the *Sunday Times* magazine's 'A Life In The Day' column.

24 October 2008

I love my cats, and I guess they think I'm okay. But I do sometimes get a very strong sense that they are purring at me, not with me.

5 November 2008

Received missing parakeet missive through letterbox. Immediately went to check cats' muzzles for feathers. Seemed clean. Parakeet in question answers to the name Charlie, talks and is 'very tame'. Religious flyers sticking out of my letterbox I can cope with of a morning. This level of emotional turmoil I cannot.

13 December 2008

Starting to regret jeering at Janet for falling off the banister earlier. Just spotted him walking towards golf bag, with distinct 'wee face'.

16 December 2008
You know your cat's got a lot of Facebook friends when he knows four cats called Chairman Meow.

4 March 2009
Have been smelling the downstairs of my house and checking for dead things for last few days. Has been a bit of a mystery. Ended up thinking 'only explanation is that there's a dead fish, being eaten by maggots, in the cat flap tunnel'. Turned out there was a dead fish, being eaten by maggots, in the cat flap tunnel.

14 May 2009
Favourite cat name of the month: F Cat Fitzgerald (from Garrison Keillor's novel, *Pontoon*).

15 May 2009
Walked across kitchen. Accidentally knocked pillowcase off radiator. Pillowcase fell onto most dignified cat, giving appearance of superheroesque 'bumcape'. Most dignified cat walked across kitchen, visibly less dignified. Confession: did not rush to retrieve pillowcase.

24 June 2009
Earlier today, I stroked my beard. Not the most riveting anecdote, I grant you. What does make it marginally more interesting is that the beard in question was false, sitting on my bedroom floor, where I'd discarded it after the previous night's fancy dress party, and at the time I had mistaken it for one of my cats.

28 June 2009
They say that some days you eat The Bear, and some days The Bear eats you. What they fail to add is that some days all that happens is that The Bear eats a tray of Sheba Rabbit and Chicken Tender Terrine, while you sit nearby, attempting to eat a jam sandwich without choking on mechanically recovered meat fumes.

17 July 2009
Friend of a friend at the Latitude music festival, in Suffolk, today: 'Oh you're the cat bloke!'
    Me (hurt): 'Well, not JUST that.'
    Logo on umbrella above my head at the time: 'PURINA ONE – FOR FELINE NUTRITION!'

20 July 2009
Have bought job lot of Felix As Good as it Looks – aka As Bad as it Smells –- cat food by mistake. In bulk. Cats looking like they might call the RSPCA.

25 July 2009
To manufacturers of Felix As Good as it Looks – aka As Bad as it Smells – cat food: I sense you tell no word of a lie (and not in a good way).

4 August 2009
Think I have just invented new foodstuff: the scromelette. Like most culinary revelations, it's hard to think why it hasn't been invented before. NB: I will not accept 'because it's just like rubbish burned scrambled eggs with one single cat hair in them' as valid reason.

6 August 2009

Odd: could swear I set a Google alert for 'cat' but it seems I must have actually set one for 'all the bad news about cats imaginable'.

8 August 2009

Ralph bit me quite hard today, when I made the unforgivable error of only using the pet mitt on him for seven minutes, instead of the twenty presumably stated as 'required' in *The Big Book of Spoilt Oversensitive Feline Idiot Therapy*. More effective than a brush, the pet mitt elicits very different responses from all my cats, but each has the common factor of being extreme. Janet mewls helplessly at its merest touch, before lying on his back and trying to bite it. The Bear runs away from it in a manner that, even for him, is notable for its campness. Bootsy and Pablo seem to simultaneously like and hate it, scarpering from it but also returning to ask for more of its sweet embrace. Ralph and Shipley just want to be mauled by it on a round-the-clock basis. I haven't tried it on myself, since I'm a bit worried about the results. In every way aside from the fact that it cost more, this current pet mitt is a cheap imitation of my original one, which was two-sided (one side tough and dimpled, the other soft and felty) and which Dee made me throw away because it had got 'too skanky'. I can see that it's effective, but I could live without the puncture wounds. When I looked down at the two small but surprisingly deep holes in my finger, I pictured a couple of furry ears and a small twitching nose above them, and was able to feel new empathy with the wretched hand that the south Norfolk vole is so often dealt in life.

17 August 2009
Many people might think it impossible for a grown feline to burst into tears. None of these people, uncoincidentally, have met my cats.

1 September 2009
Have received message from my Uncle Paul and Auntie Jayne, who woke up yesterday to find their bath-loving, black demon cat Eddie sitting upright in the bed between them, his head on the pillow and the duvet pulled up to his shoulders, 'like a little bloke'. This is perhaps as impressive as the time Paul was gardening and got a face full of next door's hose spray, only to realise the liquid in question came from Eddie, who was on the other side of the bush Paul was weeding around, marking his territory. It is, however, arguably not as impressive as the time Paul woke up to find the family hamster had escaped from its cage, crawled into bed with him and gone to sleep in his armpit.

11 September 2009
Tomorrow's *Times* newspaper includes a piece by me on corrupt ex-Taiwanese President Chen Shui-bian. Actually, that's not true. It's about cats.

14 September 2009
Watched *Whistle Down The Wind*. Saw scene with kittens in a box. Missed next three scenes as was pondering fact that kitten actors now dead.

18 September 2009

I remember those heady, footloose times, thirteen to fourteen minutes ago, when my kitchen floor wasn't completely caked in cat puke.

20 September 2009

Received letter from Italy, where my book *Under the Paw* has just been published. 'I buy your book *The Man with 24 Paws* . . . come soon in Italy . . . Thank you to love all cats like us'. I think I would like to move to Italy.

22 September 2009

The Bear just got absolutely battered by a dog in his dream. Hard to tell, but I'm sensing Yorkshire Terrier.

7 October 2009

Woke up to find a damp, half-heartedly chewed dead mouse outside my bedroom door this morning. From this, I can deduce that today is a day of the week.

1 November 2009

Bought cats wholesome, 'natural-looking' catnip mouse. Cats rejected wholesome, 'natural-looking' catnip mouse. Echoes of mum trying to convince me halva 'as nice as chocolate' but with tables turned.

17 November 2009

Think there has been a significant household misunderstanding in my house today. When I said 'cats can be gits sometimes' I wasn't granting official permission.

30 November 2009

Cats have been leaving perfectly severed vole faces and entrails outside the spare room again. Have warned my forthcoming houseguests to wear slippers.

Houseguests: 'Why's that then?'

Me: 'It's just very cold and I worry about you.'

4 January 2010

Noting the scenes inside and directly outside my house today, I cannot help but be reminded of that well-known Nordic proverb, 'Show me a dusting of snow, and I will show you a bunch of cats acting like complete and utter tools.'

15 January 2010

Saw ornamental egg on living room carpet. Thought, 'Those bloody cats have knocked that ornamental egg off the shelf again.' Picked egg up. Was real egg. Washed egg off hands.

2 February 2010

Found a note in my cat notebook which says, 'Mouse. Local Conservative Club. Second wang!' Have absolutely no idea what it means.

7 March 2010

Just rescued a duckling. I say 'rescued'. I actually lifted it off the carpet away from four bored, hot cats. It then fly-waddled into a bush.

Heavyosity

Everything had been going well for Poppy until she went to Crufts – at least, that was the way her owner, Sandra, saw it. Poppy had been following her diet and exercise programme for six months and, while there had been a few minor transgressions, the odd small piece of ham here and there at dinnertime, the improvement had been noticeable and Poppy's weight had dropped from 58 kilograms to 53.5. What better way to reward her, Sandra thought, than to show her off in the Pedigree Awareness category of the world's biggest canine gathering?

So maybe passers-by did sometimes stop and say that Poppy's back was so big a person could eat their dinner off it; what of it? No one at the world's biggest dog show could deny she was a fine specimen, despite those few extra pounds. It had been a terrific day – right up until the moment when Sandra returned to Poppy's pen to be told that some children had dropped a chocolate muffin into it, which five-year-old Poppy had summarily gobbled up. As Sandra pointed out, a Japanese pinto akita was never going to be a 'high-energy' dog, but it was such a shame, since Poppy had seemed happier, more alert before then.

If pushed, I would have had to confess that, until meeting Poppy, I hadn't realised that a Japanese pinto akita *was* a dog. If anything, I'd have pegged it as a small car, renowned for its tight turning circle and the smart, bespectacled and be-suited women populating its marketing campaign. I wasn't sure exactly what the dimensions of Poppy's turning circle were, but I would guess from looking at her now that they wouldn't have impressed the presenters of *Top Gear*. She looked like an unusually large Alsatian crossed with a posh skittle. These, however, were observations I was careful to keep to myself under the fraught circumstances.

Sitting across from me in a chilly room in Liverpool University's rather touchingly named Small Animal Hospital, Sandra put her head in her hands. 'It must have been the muffin, mustn't it?' she asked Dr Alex German, the founder of Britain's first ever weight-loss clinic for pets, rhetorically. Poppy, a dog that Sandra had told me was 'clever' and hence 'easily bored', sat passively at her feet, alongside the scales that had just revealed she had gained a kilogram since her last visit. To me, this was a whole new concept in weight gain. Perhaps a whole basket of muffins could do this much damage, but *one*? Really? 'Yes, definitely the muffin. There was nothing else,' Sandra continued. Nothing apart from the daily 370g of Royal Canin food – a special formula prescribed by German to provide Poppy with protein, vitamins, minerals and L carnitine, an ingredient that speeds up the metabolism and preserves lean tissue during weight loss.

But suddenly Sandra seemed unsure. She knew she had been strict with Poppy, feeding her separately from her other dogs and walking her for up to an hour on weekdays and two hours every weekend, losing two stone herself in the process. But there had been signs that her husband, Charles, wasn't quite so committed. German had already had to reprimand him, on a recent visit to the clinic, for letting Poppy help herself to large pieces of leftover chicken. Now Sandra became suddenly worried about further indulgences. 'He's just a bit soft,' she said. 'He feeds her the way a granny would feed a small child.'

A few moments later, after Sandra had left, explaining as she did to Poppy that they 'must have some serious words with Daddy', Alex shook his head. 'This happens every so often with joint owners. One will be committed to the programme, but the other just won't take it seriously. What people have to realise is that to get your pet to lose weight is hard work. It takes all-round discipline.'

I'd been sent to meet Alex by the *Daily Telegraph* newspaper, who'd asked me to write an article about the phenomenon of fat pets, after a report had come out suggesting that 40 per cent of Britain's cats and dogs were overweight, and Petplan, a company that provides insurance for 80,000 pets in the UK, had announced a 60 per cent surge in obesity-related claims for pet health problems in the previous five years. According to Alex, the people of Britain were 'taking less exercise and eating more meals' which meant our pets were getting less exercise and more titbits.

During the course of my research, I'd spoken to the owners of Benji, a formerly gargantuan ginger and white Tom from Hampshire whose profound inertia left him persecuted by the animal they referred to as his 'brother', a rabbit who would dive-bomb his enormous frame when he was least expecting it. I'd also heard the story of a dog who 'couldn't get enough' of the faecal pellets that his owner's rabbit left lying around the house and a parrot who gorged itself on 'nothing but pizza and pasta'.

I had to own up to a personal interest in the story, too. I've always had a fondness for roly-poly cats and, with Winter Pablo on the rise, rather liked the idea of meeting some other family-sized moggies. If my editor had also mentioned upon commissioning me there was a chance I'd meet a giant, pizza-loving parrot, I would probably have waived my fee on the spot, but on the whole my enthusiasm for overweight pets didn't extend much further than the feline. A fat dog seemed shameful and sad, but for some reason a plump cat seemed like one of the hallmarks of any good winter living room, alongside a half-open Dickens novel, a log fire and an elderly relative snoring on an armchair with a string of Werthers Original-flavoured drool hanging from his mouth. After an hour with Alex, however, I was beginning to change my mind quite drastically.

'We had a Siamese here that should have been five kilograms but weighed more than thirteen,' he told me. 'A lot of people with overweight or obese pets just see them as cuddly. But obesity can lead to numerous illnesses, such as diabetes in cats, osteoarthritis in dogs and pancreatitis, bladder stones and cardio-respiratory and orthopaedic diseases in both.' Something – I'm not quite sure what – about his expression told me this was not the time to mention the part-joking conversation I'd had in the pub with my friend Tom not long ago about 'growing' our cats.

After Poppy had left, a black cat called Molly was brought into the room. At one point, said her owner, Michelle, Molly's stomach used to drag along the floor when she walked, which wasn't often. 'I used to poke her with a stick and she wouldn't move. She was a big fan of cheese and onion crisps and liked to eat the butter off toast, but she had really greasy fur and dandruff as well.' Molly's weight loss from 6.9 to 6.15 kilograms had left her fur loose around her shoulders. Her head seemed to belong to another, much daintier black cat. That said, unlike Smokey, the grey cat I met immediately after her, she had never looked 'like a seal', which is how her owners, Clive and Margaret from Wales, described the X-ray they were given of their pet upon first visiting the clinic. In the eight months since then, Smokey's chest had been reduced by fifteen centimetres in diameter and she had been able to get upstairs unassisted for the first time in years.

'Have you thought of holding cat aerobic classes?' Margaret asked Shelley, Alex's assistant. 'No, I think that might be a bit difficult to arrange,' replied Shelley. During this exchange, I'd been lost in a daydream about struggling to help an obese Pablo into a miniature stairlift, so there had been a satellite delay before it registered. I chuckled, belatedly, but it occurred to me that neither Margaret nor Shelley was entirely joking. Alex had, after all, earlier told me about another patient, a gluttonous two-year-old Labrador called Bruce, who regularly attended a water aerobics session in Southampton called 'Doggypaddles', held in a luxury hydrotherapy pool purpose-built for dogs.

Alex told me about the importance of exercise for cats – how they are wrongly perceived as low-maintenance animals and their need for recreation is underestimated. Flashing on a mental image of Ralph meowing his own name outside the bedroom window while Shipley angrily demanded that I wipe the rain off his back with a rose-scented tissue, I tried to think of a time when I'd perceived my cats as low-maintenance, but came up with a blank. Having recently bought them a packet of Zoom-Around-The-Room organic catnip, I also felt sure in saying they were getting a fair amount of exercise. Nonetheless, I was a little nervous as I showed Alex a picture of Pablo on my mobile phone.

Did Alex think Pablo looked overweight, I wondered.

'Hard to say, looking at this picture. I'd really need to feel around his ribs,' said Alex. A picture popped into my head of Alex feeling Pablo's ribs, and Pablo immediately rolling on his back and sticking his tongue out even further than usual, while other, more sophisticated obese cats expressed their disapproval. For the third or fourth time that day, I gave thanks that I hadn't brought Pablo to Liverpool with me.

'Come in here a moment,' said Alex, beckoning me through to his office. He double-clicked his computer's mouse and a short film appeared on his monitor showing a tortoiseshell cat hurling itself maniacally back and forth, head over heels, in front of a battery-operated toy: a yellow plastic stand with a bendy antennae protruding from it, and a small chunk of fur on the end of that. In the background, the buzz of human voices could be heard. 'That's my cat, Clarence,' said Alex. The toy, he said, was a Japanese contraption called the Panic Mouse, and had been instrumental in helping reduce Clarence's weight. To illustrate, Alex pointed to a picture on his corkboard of a younger Clarence, presumably taken around the time Clarence was most liberally exploiting the perks of his job as restaurant critic for the *Financial Times*. 'Clarence has really been a bit of a guinea pig for the whole clinic,' added Alex, who, I was slightly disappointed to find, was yet to put an actual guinea pig on his weight loss programme.

Twenty minutes after I arrived home from Liverpool, I logged on to panicmouseinc.com and, for the not inconsiderable sum of £22.99, purchased a Panic Mouse. 'Revolutionary in design, The Panic Mouse's built-in computer board signals a battery-powered motor, creating random and unpredictable 'mouse-like' movements,' I was assured by the website. 'More than just toys for cats, Panic Mouse interactive cat toys provide hours of fun for both pet and owner. The plastic wand bends and contorts, bouncing back to its original form. The illusive object of cat curiosity: an artificial fur pouch that feels and acts like a real mouse.' Two days later, as I signed for the Panic Mouse and set it down on the kitchen counter, Shipley quickly and vocally arrived on the scene, followed more languidly by Bootsy and Ralph.

It was early days, but I couldn't help asking myself the burning question that had been playing on my mind: could it really be true? Was panicmouse.com really telling the truth in saying that their toy was 'the much meowed-for answer for playful cats everywhere'?

'What's this?' asked Shipley, rubbing the side of his face on the Panic Mouse's box, then sitting on top of it in his oven-ready chicken pose. Mail time is always a time of day when Shipley feels his input, as an expert on anything pulped, is invaluable, and he will usually help me sort through packages by sitting in a cardboard box or gnawing at a jiffy bag. He also knows that I often buy him presents from a big cat toy shop called amazon.co.uk, some of which he's found very tasty, though he rarely eats them all in one go. Some of those he's enjoyed most have included Rose Tremain's *Sacred Country* and Joseph Heller's *Catch-22*, though he was not so keen on Don DeLillo's *Great Jones Street*, owing to its chewy, laminated American jacket.

'It's a Panic Mouse,' I replied. 'It's going to be really good – particularly since, after you've spent some time using it, and people pick you up, they won't say "Aaaaarrrueegh!" any more and get shooting pains going down their arms.'

'What are you talking about? This box is way too heavy and big to contain a mouse!'

'Well, if you get off the top of it, I'll open it up with this knife and show you.'

'Mweeew!' said Bootsy.

'Raaalph!' said Ralph.

I still didn't think any of my cats were obese, but since I'd returned from my meeting with Alex, I was starting to view their physical mass in a more critical light. Was that the beginnings of a tummy Bootsy was developing, and, if so, how long would her tiny frame be able to put up with it? When Ralph had been to the vet last week, was the vet just being polite by calling him 'chunky'? And was Janet's slight struggle through the cat flap just the normal movement of a larger-than-average male cat, or the beginning of a slippery slope which would end with me having to attach him to a skateboard in order for him to be successfully transported to his food dish?

By purchasing the Panic Mouse, I hoped, I had stopped the decline just in time, and sure enough, within a minute of me opening the package, my cats were making ample use of its contents. Bootsy and Pablo spent much of the next hour being vastly entertained by three of the polystyrene beads in which the Panic Mouse had been packed, with

The Bear shyly taking over during the mandatory breaks Pablo takes from any leisure activity in order to practise his neutered dry hump on Bootsy. It was also clear that the invoice that panicmouse.com had sent with the toy was to the liking of Shipley's palate.

As for the Panic Mouse itself, the results were not quite what I'd anticipated. I'd decided to begin by testing it out on Janet, who, having the IQ of cottage cheese, is usually happy to chase almost anything, not excluding his own foot fur. But as I started the Panic Mouse's antennae flicking, he gave it only the most cursory of bats, before getting down to the far more vital business of removing some deeply embedded lake scum from his tail.

Over the following weeks, Dee and I did our best to get the other cats interested in the Panic Mouse, setting the antennae at a variety of different speeds and angles, but their response was similar to Janet's. Had each of them leaned against it with a cigarette in their mouth, lifted up a foot and struck a match against one of their paw pads, they could not have shown more aloof disregard. When placed in front of it, Ralph mostly just yawned, Shipley swore indignantly at me and wandered off, Bootsy delicately and nonchalantly licked a paw, while The Bear gave me a series of the eloquent, wide-eyed 'You are joking, right?' stares that only he can quite perfect. Pablo, meanwhile, seemed downright terrified, bolting outside every time I switched the Panic Mouse on, with a look in his eyes that suggested he had seen a plastic foot soldier of the apocalypse.

I could see their point: I'm not quite sure why my cats were supposed to think that the Panic Mouse was inherently mouse-like just because somebody had painted some whiskers, eyes and big ears on its smooth yellow base. If you applied the same logic, the giant wooden fish hanging in my entrance hall, carved by my Uncle Paul, would have been driving them wild with hunger for years.

The part of the Panic Mouse the cats were intended to chase was actually more birdlike than mouse-like. Perhaps a mouse-bird hybrid was an unnatural contravention of some ancient leisure code, like manufacturing a sporting missile that was halfway between a rugby and soccer ball?

Even so, I suspected that my cats were making a special, concerted group effort to ignore it. The Panic Mouse might have been no better than lower budget, less elaborate toys, but that didn't necessarily mean it was any worse. I'm sure it wasn't just my imagination that Pablo, Shipley, Bootsy, Ralph, Janet and even The Bear seemed to be hammering home their disinterest in the Panic Mouse by playing more than usual with other, entirely random loose impediments hanging around the house. I would not have been surprised if, in a further spirit of belligerence, they had left me their own amazon.com-style customer reviews of their other discoveries, complete with star ratings. These would probably include:

1. The Dried Noodle ★★★★
'It's always one of life's letdowns when your human turns on the hob and it turns out there's nothing fish- or meat-based in the offing, but sometimes when there's boiled water involved, it's worth sticking around. After all, you never know: something brittle and magical might end up on the floor. Noodles might not taste as good as a turkey's wattle or a mouse's face, but there's really nothing finer to bat round a parquet floor on a bored Sunday afternoon – particularly when we're talking about the dried, uncooked version.

Watch, as, under the control of your deft paws, the noodle skitters across the floorboards, under chairs, stools and cabinets! *Recline*, and stare for literally hours at the curve of the dried unleavened dough! *Fantasise*, as the noodle becomes a shrew, pike, triceratops or any mythical beast you care to imagine! Forget catnip mice – these cheeky little fellas do it for me every time.' – *Janet*

2. The Random Chunk of Cardboard ★★★★★

'Most cats say boxes are best for sleeping, but that's just propaganda. And while newspapers are good for casual chewing, nothing feels finer between the teeth than a well-made bit of household packaging. Recent personal favourites include the protective shells for 'Vax Integra Carpet Washer 7652' and the latest wireless audio fm transmitter from iStuff, but nothing quite beats the timeless chewability of 'Big Yellow: This Way Up'. Tear it off in strips or chunks! Casually masticate a corner while your step-brother is curled up peacefully inside! The choices are endless . . .' – *Shipley*

3. The Rotting Pampas Grass Leaf ★★★

'The pampas grass is a double-edged sword – and I mean that literally. Given a patient, play-happy owner to hold the other end of the blade, there's nothing better for playing "Clappy Paws" with. It's hard not to appreciate the craftsmanship, as you watch it slide across a freshly mown lawn. Squint and you can even convince yourself that it's an unusually pointy-headed snake. But beware: get over-enthusiastic, and those sharp edges can sting. Not recommended for kittens under 10 weeks old.' – *Ralph*

4. The Bootsy ★★★★★

'Small but perfectly formed, the Bootsy comes in one colour (grey) and is extraordinary lifelike – both in the pained squeaks it emits as you scrag its neck, and in its habit of lying in catlike positions in the crevices of armchairs and duvets. Terrific for indolent neck-biting, back-sitting or – my personal favourite – "The Castrato Hump".' – *Pablo*

There were *some* purpose-built, man-made toys my cats still liked. A black, dusty mouse that Dee and I had bought from our local pet shop in 2001 was now in its seventh year of duty, its squeak sometimes vanishing, but then reappearing and reigniting the bloodlust of its users every time I was poised to retire it from service. There was also 'Camden': a game devised by Dee which involved draping a feather-on-a-stick toy around the neck of Bootsy, feather boa-style, as she tried to chase it, and which proved very popular with its participant, whose tastes have always run to the glitzy. Then there was the toy known only as The Thing: a small, purple item that had arrived unbidden with a package of over-priced German cat food a month or two after the Panic Mouse.

The only real merit I could discern in The Thing was that the fur stuck to it seemed extremely – some would say disturbingly – lifelike, yet it was soon to take an unassailable lead in the race for the title of Most Mauled Cat Toy of 2008: a lead that ultimately, despite the efforts of the toy otter from Dee's childhood that Bootsy liked to kick off her favourite chair, it would never relinquish.

By this point, the Panic Mouse had been all but forgotten. I relocated it outdoors at one point, with the thought that context might be its main problem, and The Bear minced up to it quite perkily and promisingly, but in the end he just turned around, lifted his tail and unleashed a hot jet of urine into its face, while looking passionately and committedly into the furthest recesses of my eyes. Dee and I began to ask cat-owning friends if they'd like to take it off our hands, but they all had either tried a Panic Mouse before and had similarly dismal results, or were unconvinced by its merits.

I began to feel worryingly like the toy's unofficial marketeer, scouring the Internet for pictures of multi-coloured cats with it in mid-air action poses, then sending them to friends. While its batteries lived on, I couldn't quite bring myself to consign it to a cupboard, so had taken to leaving it on at night. I actually had two motives in doing this. On the one hand, I was doing an artificial version of what I'd done in the past with the real rodents my cats had hurt and discarded, and which I'd been so afraid to kill: if the Panic Mouse was somewhere else and out of its misery, then I could move on cleanly with my life. On the other hand, part of me was trying to catch the furry schemers out.

Like a lot of cat owners, I was convinced that, when I was asleep, my cats lived an entirely different life: a mixture of the downright unexpected, and the activities they stubbornly shirked in daylight. So one night about a month into the Panic Mouse's unappreciated life, having got up in the middle of the night for a glass of water, I was pleased to hear what sounded unmistakably like a paw being thrashed against its artificial fur pouch. As I crept towards the sound, I felt bad to have doubted Panic Mouse's manufacturers. The furry pouch *was* 'the much meowed for illusive object of cat curiosity' after all!

I suppose it wasn't a surprise to see that the cat enjoying the illusive object of cat curiosity was Pablo. Pablo has never had the duplicitous nous of my other cats, to say the least, and his attitude to the Panic Mouse from the beginning had been terror rather than indifference. Clearly he'd just needed time to work out its merits.

I padded carefully towards him but something looked a bit odd about Pablo. The Panic Mouse was supposed to make cats thinner, but if I wasn't mistaken, Winter Pablo looked even larger than usual. Lying upside down, he was a veritable puddle of cat, spilling across the floor. For all his intermittent bulk, Pablo had always had a pointy sort of face, compared by many to that of the celebrity chef and smallholder Hugh Fearnley-Whittingstall, but now his jowls looked hideously stretched, his expression blank and moon-like. As he spotted me at the periphery of his vision, I saw none of the usual eagerness or nerves in his countenance, just something dopey and dazed.

There's a familiar moment when you taste some crisps you've picked out of a bowl at a party that you thought were one flavour, but are actually another flavour, and momentarily baulk at them. It doesn't matter if you actually like the flavour of the crisps you have in your mouth; merely because you've thought they are a different flavour, the world momentarily spins on its axis, and everything you have ever believed turns upside down. Looking at Pablo, I experienced a similar moment. Of course, when you've realised your mistake, and that the crisps in your mouth are actually harmless, and, possibly, even a flavour you liked just as much as the flavour you mistook them for, the world stops spinning. It was an equivalent moment to this that I subsequently experienced, as I realised that Pablo was in fact

Samson, the ginger cat owned by Ruby, the old lady who lived across the road.

I'd pretty much fallen in love with Samson from the first moment he'd trespassed on our property, three years earlier, and there would have been a good chance I might have stolen him had I not been just slightly uncomfortable with the idea of depriving elderly widows of their life companions. Since those days, Dee and I had realised that, for the sake of our bank account and Samson's gut, it was a good idea to put the biscuits on a different floor to our original cat flap, and Samson hadn't been around so much, although I still saw him at Ruby's house when I went there to swap books with her, or to pick her up before driving her to the occasional classical music recital in Norwich.

When Dee and I had moved into the Upside Down House, in 2004, Ruby had been the first neighbour to introduce herself to us and make us feel welcome. When I thought of the phrase 'perfect neighbourhood', the picture that came into my mind was essentially a dozen versions of her, trotting industriously along a quiet street, grey hair immaculately coiffed, umbrella in hand. Ruby, a former physiotherapist, was eighty-five when I first met her, but her hands, feet and mind were lively. She read *The Times* from cover to cover every day, expressing her dismay at the paper's newfound obsession with celebrity, and at least one thick novel every week. Her husband had passed away over two decades earlier and her three sons lived far away, but her life was a full one, and I don't think I've ever known anyone so frustrated by the limitations of old age.

Ruby raged with particular force against her failing

hearing. This did not mean she conquered it, but you could tell she was having an almighty go at doing so.

'Dee saw Samson over by our bins again the other day,' I might say to her. 'She was a bit worried about him crossing the road so she brought him over and put him in your garden.'

'What? The black one? I wondered if that was yours,' she would reply. 'It comes over quite a lot.'

'No, Samson,' I would say. 'He was across the road again.'

'I'm sorry. This blasted hearing aid isn't really working. Dreadful thing. Tell me again.'

'Oh, sorry Ruby, I'll speak up a bit. I said, "Dee saw Samson by our bins again the other day. She brought him back over the road, though, to make sure he's safe."'

'OH, I understand now. Yes, well, it's dreadful what they've done to the fountain. If I was the Petersons at number eighteen, I'd complain.'

Despite these occasional misunderstandings, an unlikely, not-quite-close daytime bond grew between Ruby and me. She was an octogenarian church group regular with a passion for Debussy and Marks & Spencer thermal wear. I was a thirtysomething bloke with unruly hair and stubble and a large collection of prog rock LPs. Yet, somehow, in our cats, we found common ground leading us to other topics.

Ruby was extremely good at keeping me up on local gossip, none of which she delivered maliciously. That some of this gossip was three decades or more out of date somehow added to its intrigue. I was absolutely scandalised, for example, to hear of a rumour that the hospital that had been next to my house's to-be-built-on plot in the late 1950s had been closed down because 'all of the doctors and nurses were having their wicked way with one another'. For

Ruby, time had evidently not dimmed the impact of either this, or a more contemporary scandal – in 1973, I think she said it had happened – about a man at a local garden centre who, when out of his overalls, liked to wear his wife's tights, knickers and lipstick.

As Ruby relayed this information to me, or interrogated me about my latest piece of journalism for her favourite newspaper, Samson was always in close attendance, sitting on one of our laps or on the Axminster in front of Ruby's log fire, in a pose that brought to mind the phrase 'Beached Mammal: Miscellaneous'. He was a model of placid gingerness, and it was owing to this that, when Dee and I decided to get our own ginger cat, we headed directly to the same rescue centre where Ruby had acquired Samson.

Pablo turned out to be a sunny simpleton, but Samson was something more: a simpleton who appeared to be permanently, hopelessly stoned. When you called or stroked him, he would look at you in apparent slow motion, with something that only bordered on interest, yet was not in any sense disapproving. He was a silent creature, but had he been talky, like Shipley, I'm sure an inordinate amount of his sentences would have ended with the word 'dude'.

His only real concessions to animation were the fierce but well-meaning bites he would administer to his strokers. These must have been hell on Ruby's hands, but she never reprimanded him for them, which meant the paper-thin skin over her knuckles was permanently covered in purple bruises. Another measure of her love for him was the state of her seating. Ruby's big Georgian house never resembled the hideaway of an infirm person, always having an immaculate appearance and a fresh airy smell about it. The exceptions were her sofas and armchairs, which were so violently slashed, one might have imagined a special task force of inept policeman had recently cut them open in a drugs raid. I was well aware of what kind of damage sharper-clawed cats such as The Bear and Bootsy could do to my own sofas, but each of them would have had to buy their own Swiss Army knife and work non-stop for a month to have achieved anything even close to this.

I'm not sure why I hadn't thought of Samson immediately when I was trying to find a taker for the Panic Mouse. Maybe, because of his somnolence and sheer bulk, I unfairly wrote him off. The morning after I caught him playing with it, I excitedly told Dee that I had finally found a good home for it. But she explained that she had forgotten to tell me that, the day before, she had promised it to a work friend, Louise. I wanted to campaign on behalf of Samson, but I knew Louise and her boyfriend Daniel had recently acquired a new, playful, young stray kitten, Garvey, and stealing a toy from an orphan didn't seem any more ethical than stealing one from a grown adult. I was also secretly confident that the Panic Mouse would be returned.

I saw Ruby a couple of times in the month after that: first when she asked me for a copy of my latest book, and then again, a couple of weeks later, when she and her friend Gaynor knocked on my door to tell me she'd lost Samson.

'How long has he been gone?' I asked.

'Oh, at least three and a half hours now!' replied Ruby.

I'd been known to start worrying myself into circles after as little as twenty-four hours without a sighting of The Bear, and always been told by Dee that I was overreacting, but Samson was clearly a more homely companion. I joined the search party, combing my house and garden, and alerting a couple of other neighbours, then, after a final look behind the back of our wheelie bin, where Samson had often been spotted in the past, loitering with a confused expression on his face, I headed over to Ruby's to give her my glum news.

'Oh, don't worry,' said Gaynor, answering the door. 'We've found him now. He'd gone to sleep under the duvet. He doesn't normally put his head all the way under. Ruby's gone up there for a nap with him now.'

I was away on work trips quite a lot in the time immediately after that, and there were no more sightings of Samson around the bins, or on the bottom floor of the house. Ruby was almost ninety, and had looked tired and been less talkative when I'd seen her, but it was an enormous shock to receive a phone call a month later from her son, Charles, announcing that she'd died. Ruby had only found out she had cancer a couple of weeks earlier, probably around the time Samson had done his disappearing act, but its progress had been swift. Having given Charles my commiserations and told him what a wonderful neighbour she'd been, my thoughts turned to Samson.

'Oh. He's still here,' said Charles. 'Moping about. Would you like to take him off our hands?'

When people ask me how I end up with so many cats, I often shrug and tell them, 'I'm not sure. They just seemed to keep wandering in off the street.' It's an answer that's served me well, and which manages to conveniently sidestep a large amount of flaws in my character, but it's also a fabrication. To a greater or lesser extent I've sought out all of my cats. Had I lived in houses where strays had actually wandered in off the street, I might not even be writing this now, since my laptop would probably be so bunged up with cat hair the keyboard would no longer function.

Now I was facing a major test of the kind I'd managed to avoid. On one hand, how could I not want Samson to be part of my household? He'd had me at 'meow'. Quite apart from the fact that he looked great on a sofa, his vacant, laid-back aura could, I felt, only have a calming influence on all eight of us. In my anthropomorphically inclined mind, I saw it as a little bit like having a Bodhisattva move into our spare room. But Dee and I had told each other that half a dozen cats was our absolute limit. Sometimes six could already feel like sixteen, and, with Pablo and Ralph's race war continuing apace, it would surely be perilous to add another ginger element. Recently, both Pablo and Ralph had begun to spray drops of some form of dark orange sub-stance around the cat flap. I couldn't be sure, but instinct told me it wasn't a special peach and rum punch they'd mixed on the quiet in the kitchen in happy unison. Much as I would like to deny it, were we to take on Samson, it's pos-sible that the question 'How much piss is in our basement?' would only fully be answered by another question: 'How much piss is in our cats?'

A person might imagine that by writing about cats professionally, he would suddenly be in the know regarding people who were in the market for a new cat. In fact, the opposite is true: I tend to be *very* in the know about cats needing homes, but rarely aware of anyone willing to offer them one. Dee and I thought long and hard about potential new owners for Samson, and made a few enquiries, but came up with a blank. We'd just about started to make plans to rearrange our domestic surroundings specifically to cater for ginger-tabby apartheid and abandon ourselves to a future of shredded sofas when Dee remembered Louise and Daniel.

It was a long shot. Louise and Daniel owned two cats, Ellie and Daisy, but until a few weeks ago had owned three. Garvey was, in their words, 'a gorgeous long-legged tabby and white kitten' who'd wandered in to the technical college where Daniel worked and immediately won over the pupils and staff, none more so among the latter than Daniel. Daniel had made extensive enquiries in the local area in an attempt to find his owner, left information at local rescue centres, to no avail. Meanwhile, he and Louise had taken Garvey home, where he had quickly secured the approval of Ellie, Daisy and their West Highland Terrier, Rosie, and attacked his new Panic Mouse toy with an enthusiasm belying some of the bad press the contraption was receiving elsewhere in the locality.

Garvey wasn't actually called Garvey at this point, but Daniel, in particular, had developed such a soulful, masculine bond with him that he felt it was only right that he should name him by the surname of the lead singer of his favourite soulful, masculine indie rock band, Elbow. He'd been living with Louise and Daniel for a whole week – enough time for them to think of Garvey as theirs, or, rather, themselves as Garvey's – when Garvey's original owners arrived at Daniel's workplace to claim him, having been alerted by the RSPCA. Daniel and Louise then had to cope with the distress of transporting him back to a council flat and watching him being roughly scragged by the owner's three-year-old son. 'It turned out his name was really something rubbish like Fluffy,' Daniel recalled.

I sensed Daniel and Louise's dynamic as an animal-loving couple was not dissimilar to that of mine and Dee's: on the surface of it, Louise, as the female, and an employee of an animal charity, was the soppy one, but penetrate that surface, and it was Daniel who was the most cut up about Garvey's departure. Not long before that, the couple had lost another cat, Murphy, to jaw cancer, and hearing Daniel talk about him made me wonder if I had encountered the ultimate clandestine Cat Man. Murphy's scraggy, moth-eaten mum had come out of nowhere one day, and sat on Daniel's chest when he was on his back, working on the undercarriage of his Alfa Romeo, and never left, giving birth to Murphy a few months later. As Daniel put it near-tearfully, he was with Murphy 'for his first breath, and his last'. That Daniel and Louise took a while before deciding to come and meet Samson was almost certainly down to the question of whether Daniel could let himself in for any more feline-related heartache.

I met them at the door of Ruby's house. The place felt as warm and congenial as ever, and it was hard to believe we wouldn't find the owner in the living room on her favourite armchair, deeply ensconced in a well-thumbed copy of *The Mayor of Casterbridge*. As Charles showed us in, I immediately found myself assuming a role somewhere between estate agent, cat PR officer and museum tour guide. 'This,' I almost said, 'is the kitchen. As you can see, it's a good size, and there's room to extend. Over there you'll see the top of the fridge, where Samson used to sit and look down on Ruby, as she tried to solve *The Times*' Sudoku puzzle.' As we passed by the stairs, I had half a mind to turn up them, to show Daniel and Louise the bed where Samson had hidden on the day Ruby lost him, before remembering it wasn't my house.

When I'm introducing two separate groups of friends, I have an annoying habit of doing subtle marketing for each, like a five-year-old forcing a couple of teddy bears to kiss, and in this case the tendency was exaggerated. I found it hard to hide how much I wanted Samson and Daniel and Louise to hit it off.

We found Samson in the living room, sitting staring blankly at the coal fire. 'Samson, this is Daniel and Louise,' I said, and, in slow motion, he looked up at us. Was that an extra hint of melancholy I detected in his moonlike gaze? I thought it was. There is an argument to be made that the reason Ralph was sluggish in the two months after his brother, Brewer, was run over and killed, was that it just happened to be a period when he was eating a large amount of poor-quality rats, but I believe that his mood was entirely down to his bereavement. I remain convinced that animals are capable of mourning, and that this extends to their relationships with humans. Of course Samson would be lost without Ruby! Cat–human relationships did not get any closer than theirs.

Feeling this more acutely, and perhaps being prompted to go for the hard sell, I picked Samson up and passed him to Daniel, along with his favourite brush.[3] Samson had always been keen on being brushed, but there was a touch of sado-masochism about the process: that 'I like this! I don't like this! Do more of it!' emotion that so many cats seem to be feeling during so many of their leisure pursuits. After expressing such sentiments via the medium of a bite on Daniel's knuckles, and receiving a disciplinary tap on the nose, he began to calm down slightly, especially when Daniel discovered his favourite spot: the side of his lip.

---

[3] Samson's favourite brush, that is; I didn't know if Daniel had a favourite brush and, if he did, it was none of my business.

Shipley is also enthusiastic for the lip-stroke, and if he doesn't get a chance to rub his face across my hand first thing in the morning, will essentially shout abuse at me for the following three hours. Shipley, however, has never liked a brush running across the side of his mouth. If someone put some bristles against my lips, I'd be tempted to give them a good slapping, but nothing made Samson happier. With that itch scratched, he fell into a deep sleep on Daniel's lap, while Louise gently stroked his scruff.

Selecting a cat isn't like selecting a car or a house. Perhaps it might be sensible, after meeting certain moggies for the first time, to go back home and have a deliberating period before making a final decision, but etiquette can make such a course of action tricky. After all, what are you going to go home and discuss? The cat's resale value? Whether that wear and tear on its paws is going to prove a long-term problem? In a situation where a member of the cat's extended family is present, there's also the worry about offending.

Daniel and Louise would later tell me that from the moment Samson fell asleep, they knew they wanted him to be theirs, but at the time when they announced that they intended to take him home, I worried that they felt pressured, concerned about wasting Charles' time.

'Are you sure you don't want to go away and think about it for a couple of days?' I asked. Had my public relations drive been too strong? In the last few minutes, I'd begun to see Samson through different eyes. I'd used phrases like 'docile', 'affectionate' and 'big dribbling sopball' when describing him to Louise and Daniel. But, at root, had I just pushed them into getting an overweight cat with an overzealous jaw and a bad habit of ripping up sofas?

With Louise and Daniel's decision made, Charles began to gather up Samson's possessions. These included four large bags of cat biscuits, two brushes, some form of special cat doormat, around four feather-on-a-stick toys, six or seven catnip mice and fish. We were all surprised enough to see Charles making a second journey to what he called 'The Samson Cupboard', and by the third trip, which yielded a cat play-centre the size of a small dollhouse, a ceramic like-ness, several cat books and what I can only describe as the first feline skateboard I had ever seen, there seemed little doubt that what we were dealing with here was the most loved cat in Norfolk.

'Oh yes,' said Charles, as, wedged up to our chins with paraphernalia, we made our way to Daniel and Louise's car. 'It's not essential, and naturally it's entirely up to you, but I thought I'd just let you know that he has been used to get-ting at least one chicken wing every day.'

A fortnight later, a memorial was held for Ruby at her house. There was little elbow space anywhere downstairs, and almost every neighbour and friend I'd met at Ruby's popular end-of-year neighbourhood parties was present. On mantelpieces and tables sat a selection of photographs of her. In these, she always looked bright-eyed and happy and was more often than not holding a cat. Other moggies from her past – many of them also ginger, and impressively uphol-stered – were pictured, but Samson had the edge on them, and I would estimate that scattered around the house, his image could be spotted a couple of dozen times. Every time I turned round to speak to another person, I was asked the same question: 'How's Samson getting on?'

Fortunately, I'd been to Daniel and Louise's house just the night before, so was able to provide a positive answer, without too much sugarcoating, which, only a few days previously, might not have been the case.

'It's more tense than a Gaza negotiating table here,' Daniel had told me after Samson's first night at his new home. 'We're teetering on the brink of peace with a unilateral cease-claw from Ellie and Daisy.' Samson, it transpired, had no respect for the social hierarchy that put Ellie at the top of the animal household, Daisy second, Rosie the dog third and any newcomer a distant fourth. He spent much of his first twenty-four hours hiding behind the sofa, and was reportedly finding the laminate floors, surround sound hi-fi system and lack of coal fire 'confusing'.

On day two he'd attempted to jump up onto a dining chair to get to where the cat food was kept, missed his footing and dragged the seat pad down on top of him. Louise had found him lying upside down, with the cushion still on him, and an expression that seemed to communicate the statement: 'How did I get here, and can you help?' Piled unappetisingly on top of this hardship was his new chicken-wing-free, dry-food-only diet.

But by the time of my visit, Samson seemed, if not comfortable with his new environment, then at least less defeated by it. Ellie and Daisy had begun to realise that, though a far less intelligent creature than them, prone to making plenty of faux pas in the arena of catiquette, he was a maker of love, not war (though thankfully not in the Pablo and Bootsy sense). And, as he plodded over and plonked himself down on top of me on Daniel's sofa, did I detect just a slight difference in weight?

Having conveyed this information, in the most positive

terms, to Ruby's mourners, I moved into the kitchen, where
I found Gaynor, and Ruby's former cleaner, Barbara. Both
were lifelong cat owners, and talked fondly about Samson's
habits: the way he never seemed to drink from his water
bowl, but instead liked to splash and stir its contents with
one foraging paw; his immense need to be in any room containing a human. This led Barbara to talk about Bonzo, the
naughty yet faithful cat she'd had in her early years in
Norfolk, who'd liked to walk, unsummoned, to church every
Sunday with her, her two children and the family Labrador,
and who had once spent a terrified night stuck in the
vestibule with the spirits of more pious felines.

This afternoon was a celebration of Ruby – her commu-
nal spirit, her sprightly erudition, the misunderstandings
caused by her bad hearing, even – but it was inevitably also
a celebration of the cats who'd kept her company, and made
her solitary final years so much less solitary. On my way to
the door, another neighbourly couple – a curly-haired laughing woman and her husband, a bald landscape gardener I
wanted to call Roy, even though his name was John –
stopped me and asked me about Samson's whereabouts.

'Oh, our daughter was terribly worried about him,' they
said. 'She's going to be so relieved. We would have taken
him ourselves if he hadn't found a home.' So here was the
confirmation: Samson had a fan club.

Before I left, Charles handed me a plastic bag. 'I forgot to
give you these,' he said. I'd not felt tearful once since Ruby
died, perhaps because so much positivity surrounded her
life, very nearly until the very end, but what I found inside
the bag made my throat catch: six coasters, all emblazoned
with a slightly faded photograph of Samson, looking never
more puddle-like, gazing up blankly but lovingly at the

camera – or, more likely, at the fresh chicken wing in the other hand of the person holding it.

I've only seen Samson once since then. It was several months later, and he was a far slimmer figure. As he lumbered across Daniel's laminate floor, he had a look of a cat wearing a big ginger jumper. In certain more unfeeling human circles, the flesh around his arms might have been described as 'bingo wings'. But he retained the slowness of a big cat.

In the time since then, Daniel has kept me up to date on his progress. Though he's lost more weight, he's still big enough to be seen from space. That is to say: when Daniel logged onto Google Earth to look at a picture of his house, he noticed a large ginger spillage in the corner of the driveway clearly visible as Samson.

As winter comes on, Samson spends most of his time curled up in Rosie's dog bed, but he's also prone to wander off for periods of a day or two, then return, covered in mud or oil, to calmly inquire about that evening's menu. Daniel's theory is that he has a special passion for exploring garden sheds, but when their owners come to close them, he doesn't have the speed or ingenuity to remove himself from them that other cats might, though always seems to land on his feet – even if this is rarely in a literal sense.

The arrival of Daniel and Louise's first child, Molly, does not seem to have fazed Samson. His biting is not quite as overzealous as it was, though can sometimes lead Daniel to turn up for work looking like he's been self-harming. His enthusiasm for the Panic Mouse remains undaunted. One of Daniel's Samson emails included a link to some video footage of one of his attacks on the unfortunate battery-operated beast, as in the background the Kaiser Chiefs sang 'I Predict a Riot', a song which only slightly gave the impression of mocking the actions it sound-tracked. I'm not sure that Dr Alex German would have been too impressed with Samson's performance. There's a break in the middle for a daydream. There are some fairly busy skills from the front paws, but the posterior doesn't really join in. That, though, is perhaps the eternal nature of Samson: business in front, party in the back. A sort of feline version of the mullet haircut.

I gave Daniel Samson's coasters, but, somehow, in the process, one was left in my living room. I keep meaning to post it back, but Daniel has told me not to worry about it, so it stays on the coffee table. Shipley isn't supposed to sit on this table, but then I'm not supposed to eat fizzy cola bottle sweets: I still do, and there's not much anybody's ever been able to do about it. He rarely sits on the surface itself, as he prefers his posterior – still large, but not dangerously so, by Alex German standards – to be cushioned by a placemat or a coaster. It's perhaps my imagination, but he does seem to spend much of his time sitting on Samson's face.

'Dream on,' I tell him. And, settling down, that's perhaps exactly what he does: dozing off into a parallel world where he is the fattest, the coolest, and ginger cats crumple and submit at the terrifying, descending sight of his formidable, amply cushioned bottom.

Animals I Have Considered Stealing. Number Two: Grumpy Bat

NAME:
George the Bat (unconfirmed).

OCCUPATION:
Various posts as Back-Up Haunter, Fake Undead, and Session Spook, Office of British Hauntings, East Anglian Division, 2009–10.

HOME:
The Hellmouth, South Norfolk, UK ('Second left after the BP Station, you can't miss it, if you see the electrical wholesalers on your right you've gone too far . . .')

BRIEF CV:
Brought in by Pablo and abandoned upside down near cat flap, apparently unchewed, presumably on the grounds of

being 'one of them unlucky ghostmouses'. George looked a bit dead at first, then began to silently scream at me, with a face even more expressive and strangely human than that of Gizmo from *Gremlins*, before flying up to perch on the ledge of the sliding doors in the living room. Here, he proceeded to make chuntering noises. These, while on first hearing are easy to mistake for pure panic at being in an unfamiliar environment, soon came to feel like judgements cast down from on high: not just on Pablo, Shipley and Bootsy, all of whom were watching sceptically from below, but on me, my new brightly coloured t-shirt from the sale rack in H&M, and even, ultimately, the copy of *Frampton Comes Alive!* I had left out on the dining table. George was eventually captured in a 'Golf: Violating the Rules of Fashion for 300 Years' novelty coffee mug and released gently back into the wild.

PROS:
Constant griping good for stamping out complacency, both personal and cat-based: 'Are you going to be nice and shut up, Shipley, or do you want me to go and get the bat?' Tremendously effective shoulder accoutrement of the 'people might not notice it at first, but when they do they won't stop talking about it' variety. Potentially awesome weapon to send through the bedroom windows of sleeping enemies on recondite ear-whispering missions.

CONS:
Grumpiness. Guilt trips. Constant conversations in the 'What's wrong?' 'Nothing . . . I'm FINE' ilk. Public appearances leading to misunderstandings with overzealous Goths. Unresolved heartbreak over the The People Sheep could get in way of Making a New Start.

Put Your Money on a Pony

After everything that eventually happened between us, it would probably be a bit too easy for me to say now that I could tell Boris was a problematic sort right from the moment I first set eyes on him. I'll also admit that there have been times that I've not been the best judge of character on first impressions. But I can remember that in this particular instance the alarm bells did ring unusually loudly, right from the off. I know that there are those who were there at the time who will say that that's rubbish, that I'm imposing a non-existent narrative on unconnected events. And if that is their opinion, I accept it. It is wrong, but I accept it. I was there, and I know what I saw and heard.

The first time I met Boris would have been in the summer of 2007, on one of those perfectly cloudless, friend-packed, not particularly goal-orientated days that are ten-a-penny in your youth but become all too precious in your thirties: a day when everyone is wrapped in a collective mood that's lethargic, just slightly giggly, and any future or past more than twelve hours distant seems temporarily immaterial.

Even though Dee and I had messed up our map-reading on
the way to the stables, putting Steve and Sue and Karl and
Naomi, in the car behind us, and Leo, in the car behind
them, through a u-turn assault course and making everyone
half an hour late, nobody seemed to hold it against us. We
were set to have a picnic on Holkham beach later that afternoon, one of the most spectacularly beautiful spots in
Britain, let alone Norfolk, and everyone was excited.
Everyone except Boris, who, from pretty much the second
we got out of the car, mainly just grumbled and dragged his
feet. One thing was for sure: from the way he was acting,
nobody would have suspected *for a moment* that I'd been
generous enough to refrain from asking him to go halves on
the olives and salami that we'd brought from the grocers in
Aylsham.

Back when I was a teenager, I had a habit of pulling
leaves off trees and bushes as I walked past them. I know it
was wrong, and I've grown out of it. Such low-level vandal-
ism is just about forgivable in a thirteen-year-old, but Boris
was mature enough to know better and I'm not kidding
when I say he stopped at almost every bit of foliage we
passed and yanked a piece off it. We're talking quintessential, malevolent, adolescent boredom.

Then there was the moment when Naomi pointed out
the stable door which concealed the gelding called Conker,
and said how it was funny because, the way his name on the
door was written, it actually looked more like 'Cancer' and
Boris just sort of snorted derisively, like he was above all of
us. Even if he hadn't thought it was funny, it wouldn't have
cost him anything to laugh, just for the sake of Naomi's
feelings.

Dee often finds excuses for that kind of behaviour on

behalf of the likes of Boris, and maybe Boris, being the one true local among us, was looking at the situation from another angle, taking the environment for granted. But the way I saw it, we were in one of the prettiest parts of North Norfolk, the sun was shining, hares were leaping in the fields, and you'd have to be a singularly ungracious, stubborn individual not to give in and bask in the good vibrations.

'I think he's a bit of a git,' I said to Dee, careful not to let him hear me.

'I can't believe you would say that,' whispered Dee. 'Give him a chance.'

'He's really truculent. And to be perfectly frank, he smells. I can't see myself even staying friends with him after this.'

'You never know. You might grow to like him.'

It really wasn't that I had anything against the way Boris looked. He was pretty easy on the eye, in a hirsute kind of way, and seemed to know it. I also wasn't really intimidated by his handsomeness. I mean, I was actually a bit taller than him, although I could tell, when I stood near him, just from the way he was carrying himself, that he'd kidded himself into believing he had a couple of inches on me.

Mostly, I just felt sorry for Steve, whose bad luck it had been to end up riding Boris. Steve is a very confident guy, with a sharp and notoriously filthy sense of humour, who'll often be at the helm of the conversation in whatever room he's in, but we were in Boris's kingdom now, and Boris wasn't going to let him get the better of him. From where I stood with Leo, we had a good view of Boris's truculence in full effect – the leaf munching, the dawdling, the ultra-sarcastic 'harrumphing', the refusal to respond in the slightest as Steve pulled on his reins – and the two of them had dropped well behind the rest of the party.

The original plan had been for Steve, Sue, Karl, Naomi, Dee and me to go riding together, but then, late on, Leo had called, and it turned out the stables did not have an extra horse available for him to ride, so, rather than leaving Leo on his own, I'd dropped out, forfeiting the fee I'd paid for my own ride.

'Are you absolutely sure?' everyone had asked me, and I'd gladly received the sympathy, subtly playing up my martyr-dom. In truth, I was ecstatic. In the handful of times I'd ridden before, I'd far from mastered it, and remained nerv-ous around horses. Horses, meanwhile, were fully aware of this, and, I was convinced, had a habit of goading me accordingly.

I knew Dee loved horses when I first met her, but I wasn't aware of quite how much until our second holiday together, in Devon, when she asked me to stop the car so she could say hello to some of the indigenous ponies that roam across Dartmoor. Before long, three of them were in the front seat with me, eyeing me beadily and chewing the steering wheel. The steering wheels on Ford Focuses from the 1999–2001 era are a bit rubbery and no great pleasure to pass through your hands, but that didn't mean saliva and bite marks were going to improve their design. Dee, however, seemed unconcerned, and was standing out-side the car simultaneously enclosing two of the other ponies in her arms, with a gummy, toddler-like grin on her face.

'Give them a hug,' she said. 'Don't be scared.'

'But they've got such big teeth,' I replied.

'They're not going to bite you.'

'How can you tell? I mean, look – this one's just about to start gnawing on the handbrake as we speak.'

'I can't believe you're so scared of a few little ponies.'

The time must come in any honest relationship when a person must reveal the secrets from his past, so that night in the cottage we were renting for the week, I told Dee the truth: that, as an eleven-year-old, playing football in the back field behind my parents' house, I had been chased by a giant black mare, only managing to dive over the fence, into the garden of a derelict neighbouring abode, a second before the horse crashed into the railings behind me. I thought I'd made a pretty good job of conveying the true, permanently scarring horror of the experience, even adding a bit of steam coming out of the black mare's nostrils, but she seemed unmoved.

'That sounds very odd,' she said. 'Horses don't often chase people. At least, not for no reason.'

'Of course they do!' I said. 'You see it in films. Like that one with John Wayne, where he has to round them all up with the hippie cowboys, who he doesn't get on with, and then they all make friends.'

'Were you kicking the ball near the horse?'

'No. Not at all.'

'How far away is "not at all"?'

'Twenty-five yards? I can't remember. It occurred in the early part of 1987!'

'That's way too close. You must have scared it.'

'But it was the field where I always used to play football. I staged reruns of the 1986 World Cup Quarter Final in it, but with Lineker's last-ditch attempt on goal going in instead of missing, and me playing Lineker. There had been horses in the field before. *They'd* never had any problem with me. This horse was totally new. It wasn't even its field.'

'It's always the horse's field. That's the rule. You should know that.'

Over the following years, in sporadic bursts, Dee did her best to help me get over my mild equine phobia. 'Once you've actually been on a horse,' she said, 'you'll feel completely different about them.' Trusting her word, one day in 2004 I followed her into the darkest recesses of the Norfolk countryside, to a riding school behind a campsite. I'm not sure quite what I'd expected my first proper foray into the horsey world to consist of – perhaps a big buck-toothed greeting from a bossy lady in jodhpurs called Sarah and a selection of stables, each bedecked, in perfect calligraphy, with names like Huffle Puffle and Big Mr Jones, with a neat row of long noses poking over their doors. If so, this was definitely not it. We spotted a couple of horses some way off in the distance, but other than that all we could see was a garden that had last been weeded around the time Lester Piggott won his final Derby, a rusting caravan, a couple of large sheds, and a cottage, whose once white walls were flaked and weather-beaten.

Not really knowing where else to go, we headed for the cottage, past a wooden sign with 'Strawberry's: 80p per pound!' handwritten on it, that had fallen to the ground, and which presumably belonged to Strawberry, who, if you asked me, was going to have trouble selling such a tatty piece of wood, even at that cut-down price. The front door of the cottage was wide open and, after a couple of knocks, I stepped nervously a foot or two inside and called a tentative, '*H-ello?*' A moment later a paunchy man with a comb-over, a perspiring brow and rolled-up polyester shirt sleeves appeared. We told him we'd booked a ride, he grunted, and receded once again into the dark bowels of the building. A stringy woman with sunken eyes and at least five teeth missing who could have been any age between twenty-three and forty then appeared, grunted in similar fashion, pulled on a pair of black boots, and, with a barely perceptible nod, directed us to one of the sheds. Here we were handed a pair of riding hats, then introduced to our horses: a couple of cobs called Bob and Bess.

Dee and I thought by now it was time we introduced ourselves, and we learned that our guide was called Sharon, but further information was slow in arriving. Bob the cob, who was assigned to me, was particularly furry around the ankles, even for his breed, and I'd hoped that my comment about being pleased to get a horse with flares would lighten the mood, but it failed to crack Sharon's hard shell of indifference. 'So,' I thought to myself, 'this is the woman responsible for keeping me upright on the fine line between life and death for the next two hours.'

I'm sure it's extremely uncool to ask any questions regarding safety among rural horse-loving gypsies, and I know that Dee had explained over the phone to Sharon that I was a beginner, but I couldn't prevent myself from blurting out some questions that might ensure my safety.

'So, just checking: you know this is my first time, don't you?'

'Hmyerp,' said Sharon.

'And I'm guessing you're going to tie something to Bob, which you're going to hold, to make sure he doesn't do anything dramatic?' I said.

'Hmyerp,' said Sharon.

'And I just put my foot in here and pull myself on?'

'Hmyerp. Hmyerp,' said Sharon, in a rare display of emotion.

I've spent much of my adult life defending Norfolk against prejudicial comments about incest, bestiality and farming disseminated by the kind of East London hipsters who have only ever left the capital to go to some trendy Greek island and have gained their entire knowledge about the county from a few episodes of *I'm Alan Partridge*. But if these hipsters had seen what had transpired so far on this afternoon, I doubt they would have had any of their pre-conceptions stripped away. However, at least my worries about making conversation were a temporary distraction from the fact that I was now sitting on top of a hot, heavy living creature, who was moving, and could, if the whim took him, decide to move quite a lot faster at any moment.

'You get a good view from here, don't you?' I said, as we plodded down the lane.

'Hmyerp,' said Sharon.

Being tied to Sharon, or at least being on a horse tied to Sharon, made me feel vaguely like a toddler being taken for a walk on elastic reins. I could talk very well for a three-year-old, for sure, and it vaguely impressed her, but she couldn't really perceive anything I said as being of adult substance, or worth a considered response. I pressed on in a similar vein, while, a few horse's lengths ahead of us, Dee enjoyed what was becoming her own very separate ride on Bess. Sharon continued to humour me, mostly by saying 'Hmyerp'. It was about twenty minutes later that she started whistling to herself. I recognised the tune as 'Wanted Dead or Alive', the big-haired, lighter-waving 1987 hit by Bon Jovi. In fact, I'd been listening to it myself just the previous day. It seemed a pleasingly appropriate song for today's activity, with its lyrics of cowboys and steel horses, and I couldn't stop myself asking her if she was a fan of the band.

'Me? Ooh yeah, I love them. Seen them about eleven times now.'

This was a marked improvement. Now, we were both using full syllables with one another. 'Me too,' I told her. 'I can't think of anything I'd rather do karaoke to than "Livin' on a Prayer".'

In fact, I was exaggerating a little. I did enjoy listening to Bon Jovi – a good four or five of their songs, in total – and enjoyed singing along to them in the car, but there were five hundred other rock bands I'd listen to ahead of them. On the other hand, for the next hour of my life, it was more important than anything else in the world to me that Sharon liked me, and I felt the need to press home my advantage.

'He's my perfect man, he is,' said Sharon.

'Who? Jon Bon Jovi?' I said.

'Yeah. I like his arms. He's just one of those men you know would hold a door open for you.'

'And he's got a horse, too! Even if it is a metal one. I suppose the good thing with that is that laminitis and equine flu just aren't a problem.'

At this, Sharon began to laugh, loudly and uncontrollably. The sound was throaty, with a touch of mucus, but free and jolly, and one I could never have suspected she was capable of quarter of an hour earlier.

And then she was off: telling me about Barry, the man with the lank comb-over whom we'd met back at the cottage, who was, it turned out, her brother. How, believe it or not, he'd once had hair as big as Jon's. How the two of them had got the coach down to Wembley to see the band play in 1987, without tickets, but had somehow managed to

persuade a security guard to let them in for five pounds.
About the hard times, too: their dad leaving them when
they were kids and their mum passing away two years ago,
leaving them having to gradually sell the fields off at the
back of the house to the campsite, whose owners now
wouldn't even let them ride on the adjacent towpaths. And
what did I do for a living? A writer? Really? Sharon had
written some things, too. Poems, she supposed she should
call them, though she hoped that they might get put to
music, if Barry ever picked his guitar up again, which he
should, because he was good, really good.

Earlier in the ride, Dee had periodically looked over her
shoulder with a benevolent expression on her face, but now
she looked back in a different manner entirely, perhaps jeal-
ous that she was missing out on all the good conversation.
I'd decided I was in safe hands with Sharon, and even managed an experimental trot for a few hundred yards. As I
talked to her more, something else unexpected happened:
she seemed to gain teeth.

Had I climbed atop of my second horse in the weeks immediately following that, perhaps my destiny as a rider would
have taken a different path. But because my rides together
with Dee were spaced out over a matter of months, I didn't
build the confidence to ride off the rope. Each time, I started
afresh as a beginner, and not always with a guardian as easygoing as Sharon. On holiday in Bude, in Cornwall, on a
freezing cliff top, with hands too cold to feel my reins, I
very nearly rode into a sheep, much to the consternation of
Dee and a lady called Jill with a ponytail and no time for my
nonsense. I could see the appeal of horse riding: the sense of

oneness between man and beast, the entirely new view of the surrounding countryside. But it was a oneness ordained by man; I never felt convinced that the horses I rode on *wanted* to be ridden by me. Also, much as I enjoyed being able to look over a hedge and spot a pair of hares fighting, becoming eight feet tall had not really been a major ambition of mine since shortly after my ninth birthday.

My dad once told me that being a successful supply teacher was all about 'LETTING THE KIDS KNOW IMMEDIATELY WHO'S BOSS'. I heard a similar sentiment from stable hands and riding instructors, who frequently compared their four-legged charges to stroppy adolescents. That was all very well, but I wasn't sure I had any right in showing horses who was boss. It was quite obvious to me that they were boss, and trying to pretend anything else would be just ignoring the facts.

I loved horses' nobility, their serenity. But it was something I felt correct appreciating from a distance, and didn't actually feel naturally qualified to get close to – like a rhinoceros, or the young Faye Dunaway. Certainly, people *said* it was safe to feed them an apple if you kept your palm flat as you did it, but *how could they be so sure*? It actually amazed me that Man had come to be so intimate with horses at all. If Steve Irwin had been employed to make programmes not only about taunting crocodiles but about bravely poking chestnut mares with sticks, to me that would have seemed entirely logical.

Did my horse fear all arise from that one incident when I was eleven? Perhaps. I suppose there was also to be factored in the contribution of my dad, who when I was growing up had had a habit of shouting 'WATCH OUT! YOU NEVER KNOW WHAT THEY'RE GOING TO DO!' every time we passed a horse on a country walk. But my dad had had a habit of shouting 'WATCH OUT! YOU NEVER KNOW WHAT THEY'RE GOING TO DO!' every time we passed a herd of cows on a country walk too, and I hadn't become scared of cows as a result. I might also cite a visit to the Stow-on-the-Wold Horse Fair in 2003, in which I was almost mown down by a Suffolk punch being raced by two topless adolescent gypsy boys in a buggy.

For fifty weeks of every year, Stow is the quintessential quiet Cotswolds town: a pristine place full of art galleries, perfectly arranged window boxes, delicatessens and the kind of high-end cookware shops where one might purchase a microplane cheese-grater endorsed by a celebrity chef. But in May and October, many of the galleries and shops in the town close, and the place is invaded by hundreds of gypsies from miles around, who congregate in a large field to talk, drink, hammer out cash deals on their animals – which include rabbits, dogs and donkeys, as well as horses – and catch up with old friends. It's a little bit like the Glastonbury Festival, but if the Glastonbury Festival consisted only of the Levellers, the Levellers' friends, and the random pets the Levellers' friends had accrued on their travels. The one chief difference being that most people at Stow are considerably tougher than the Levellers. In fact, their babies could probably beat up the Levellers.[4]

'Oh, we don't like *them*,' a sales assistant in a bakery told me, when I went in to buy a doughnut, before heading

---

[4] Legendarily unwashed band from the early 90s: perhaps best known for starting a trend among middle-class teenagers from well-off households for attaching the family dog to a piece of string, dreadlocking your hair, and walking around your local city pretending to be homeless.

down to the fair. 'They come running in and steal chocolate and crisps. That's why we have these.' She pointed to some specially installed wooden barriers in front of the shelves.

On my way to the fair, I spotted gangs of gypsy youths parading their horses round the town, just as teenagers in my own town might show off their pimped-up Peugeots. Some of them stood round a cob, inspecting its feet, in much the same way someone buying a second-hand car might kick its tyres beforehand. A few minutes later, upon arrival, I found two Irishmen waving fists full of fifty-pound notes in the air, and intermittently slapping one another's hands. 'Leave the luck to meeself!' one kept shouting at the other. 'Leave the luck to meeself!'

I turned to the man next to me and asked what the expression meant. 'It sort of means make your offer, then we'll see what happens,' he said, before introducing himself as Seamus, and telling me that he'd come all the way from the west coast of Ireland to sell fifteen budgerigars. 'And I'm kind of trying to get rid of her as well,' he admitted, pointing to a tiny pony about twenty yards from us, whose gums were being roughly exposed by two boys of about fifteen or sixteen, while a couple of girls, perhaps a year or two younger, in hoop earrings and tube tops, looked on, giggling in an impressed manner. 'Do you want to buy her?' She was the kind of size that even I couldn't be intimidated by, but I declined, explaining that she'd still be difficult to squeeze into the back of a Ford Focus estate.

A few years earlier, two friends of my parents, Rose and Andy, made a short-lived decision to quit their jobs in education, buy a caravan and live an alternative, gypsy-inspired lifestyle. Their dream had begun and more or less ended with a weekend at Stow, where they'd had their much-cherished family Labrador stolen and been kept up through the night by a brawl outside their caravan which finally degenerated into a full-blown axe fight.

I didn't see anything like that at Stow, but two fifteen-year-old boys with rough, outdoorsy complexions did ask me how good I was at fighting. It was a question I hadn't given much thought to since I was thirteen, so I told them that I'd been off form since my personal trainer, Big Ronnie, had died, a couple of years ago – at which they exchanged a sneering look, then began laughing at my haircut. I might have been more offended, but I was distracted owing to the fact I'd just seen a man walk past us with a live chicken in his pocket.

I'd love to be the kind of person who could confidently walk around in public with a chicken in his pocket, but it's never going to happen. I'd spend too much time glancing down at the chicken, to check it was okay, to give off the appropriately insouciant air that someone walking around with a chicken in his pocket needs. I think this also explains why I will probably never have what it takes to handle a horse. Obviously not everyone in the horse industry is quite as tough as the traders at the Stow Horse Fair, but I've noticed a certain no-nonsense attitude among horse lovers, which I know I will never possess. Many of these are people who, in 2006, Dee started to work with, after securing a job at Happy Hooves, a horse charity in Suffolk: folks who spend their working days witnessing the most horrendous equine mistreatment, yet will also look at the cold hard facts of the behaviour of one of their inmates and announce, 'I'm sorry, but that horse is being a twat.' These are animal lovers of the no-nonsense country kind who, when they refer to their 'mum's massive cock', will do so with a straight face, not for a moment imagining that anyone in the room would think they were not talking about poultry.

I have the greatest admiration for these horse rescuers, and wish I was brave and selfless enough to do what they do, but I'm not and, in their company, I'm out of my depth. I know this first-hand from the time in 2007 that I went to dinner with eight of them. I did fairly well with the conversation for most of the night, but when the talk turned to diseased horse penises, I started to get a bit lost. However, it was a pleasure to see Dee getting so involved in her new job, and I was grateful for the opportunities it gave me to further my safely distanced appreciation of horses. I even went so far as to make my own horse-themed playlist for the mornings when I drove Dee to work. Listening to The Byrds' 'Chestnut Mare', Paul Brady and Andy Irvine's 'Plains of Kildare' or Forever More's 'Put Your Money on a Pony', I would sometimes stop the car and watch the new Happy Hooves inmates.

I developed a particular obsession with Barney, a tiny, stunted, roly-poly pony of legendary grumpiness, whom Happy Hooves liked to dress in a promotional t-shirt on their open days. One day, watching him, having exhausted my horse playlist, I switched on the radio and found myself customising my own lyrics to the central, nagging riff of Deep Purple's 'Smoke on the Water': 'You, you, you/You are a horse/You, you, you . . . *are-a-horse!*'

Clearly, I was thinking about horses a lot, but Dee was thinking about them significantly more, and it was now several months since we'd been riding together. On our early rides, she had been proficient enough, but now her lessons had put her several light years away from me in ability. 'Stop the car!' she would shout as we passed a field containing a couple of bay geldings, picking up her phone and punching in Happy Hooves' number. 'Is that ragwort on the edge of that field? I can't believe it! That's going to poison them.' Our house began to fill up with saddles, boots, riding hats, a 1970s amateur painting of a white stallion. I knew she would love it if I was to join her in her favourite pursuit, and I could see her looking on enviously at the riders I slowly – even more slowly than ever, now – drove past on Norfolk and Suffolk's narrow country lanes.

One day, she arrived home, struggling with two giant polythene bags. 'Here,' she said, handing me one. 'Take this would you, and put it in the living room.'

I picked it up and felt my arms sink. 'My god. What's in them? Horse skulls or something?'

'Yep,' she said. 'They're for Dave.'

From most people's spouses, this might have seemed quite a disturbing piece of information, but I'd known Dee and her family for long enough not to be surprised. For birthdays, Dee's dad would send both of us special, surreal and wrongish constructions by a mysterious creature called The Birthday Serpent. Nobody knew where this serpent had originated from, or what it looked like, but one thing was for sure: it was a seriously messed-up snake. For my latest birthday, it had sent me a 1970s WHSmith paperclip holder box with a bar of Pear's soap inside with a dozen tiny plastic soldiers encased in it. Previous offerings included the cardboard lining to some Marks & Spencer pants, bedecked with an eerie mechanical drawing, a woman's compact sabotaged and glued with a small woodland vista and a locked wooden cigar box whose contents remained a mystery but almost certainly didn't include cigars. Dee's dad's best friend, an artist called Dave, shared, if not trumped, the serpent's macabre passions. Last time he'd visited our house, he'd developed an extreme fondness for the wicker man I'd bought from a garden centre in Swaffham, and it didn't surprise me in the slightest that his latest project would involve drawing a couple of dead horse heads.

'Won't they smell?' I asked Dee.

'No, no. No chance of that. They've been boiled and sterilised. The woman in the Dead Shed promised me.'

'The Dead Shed?'

'Yeah, it's the place where they keep all the dead horses. I virtually had to climb over a couple of dead donkeys to get to these.'

Dee had always been an amazingly unsqueamish person: a sizable fan of forensic documentaries, unflinching hospital-based dramas and serial-killer literature. Nonetheless, I was surprised. If I had been given the chance to walk around a large barn full of dead horses, donkeys and ponies, I feel sure I would have found it hard to resist blabbing about it to the person closest to me at the soonest opportunity in an overexcitable, yelping fashion. Perhaps I would have held back from an actual phone call, but wouldn't have been able to help at least sending a text message saying, 'I'm standing in a room full of horse parts!' or 'Oh my god! I just almost touched the femur of a Spotted Ass by mistake!' But for Dee it was all in the course of a day's work for the new equine-hardened her. Was this, I wondered, simply the sort of thing that happened to you when you spent too much time looking at diseased horse penises?

'Put the skulls in the cockpit for now if you like,' she said.

The cockpit was what the previous owners of my house called the glass room on the top floor, and the name has stuck. It's a room that gets very cold in winter, and very hot in summer, and one of the few rooms that the cats don't venture into. I didn't intend to leave the horse skulls in there for any length of time, but it seemed like a convenient and safe place to put them. Perhaps, as Dee said, there was no actual . . . *horse* left on the horses, but just the previous night Pablo and Janet had had great fun with a chicken carcass I'd been remiss enough to leave on the work surface, evidently taking turns to take it for the ride of its afterlife around the living room, both bathrooms and my study.

The cats were going through a lull in their killing schedule around about this point. It had been at least a month since I'd walked out of the bedroom door and stepped on a shrew's face, and almost a year since I'd had to chase a petrified moorhen around the kitchen island with a waste paper basket in my hand. So it was a surprise when, around the stairwell area, I began to smell something suspiciously like dead mouse.

I know the smell of dead mouse rather well now. It's different from the smell of dead shrew or dead vole: more . . . yellowy. This particular aroma was uncannily similar to a dead mouse I'd found last summer, too late, underneath The Bear's favourite scratching post. Yet it also had an aftersmell that was not dissimilar to that of a headless rabbit (I actually sensed the cats had not killed this themselves, though they may have munched the head, as they're all big fans of brain food) I'd found on the kitchen floor a month previous to that, and, in haste, wrapped up in a carrier bag and placed in the wheelie bin, before realising my mistake a few hot summer hours later; I'd rushed out to find the bin crawling with maggots, then had to start a complex hosing-down procedure for fear of prompting the local council to come to my house with knives to kill me. Not wishing a repeat performance, nor to gain the neighbourhood nick-name 'Maggot Man', I made it my mission to find the cause of this latest smell. But having cleared the stairwell, checked under the sofa and even behind the kickboards in the kitchen, I found nothing.

Yet The Smell remained, becoming just that bit more oozingly malevolent by the day. Were it to get any worse, I would soon probably be compelled to hammer an exploratory hole inside the wall in a last, desperate attempt to determine its origin. The Smell watched me as I worked, harrying me like the sound of a thousand evil elves whispering behind my back.

'Are you absolutely sure it couldn't be coming from the horse skulls?' I asked Dee. She was adamant that it wasn't. Dee is a remarkable font of information: a piece of human Velcro for facts. It's not just that she knows about all the stuff she needs to know about; she knows about an awful lot of stuff she doesn't need to know about as well. Want to find out about the latest techniques in DNA analysis? The secrets of maintaining your fishing tackle in a cost-effective way? She's your woman. Being well aware of this, I certainly had no reason to question her knowledge about dead horses: an area where she was, in my eyes, an acknowledged expert.

I began to smell The Smell now even when I left the house. It seemed to be with me in the car as I drove. How long, I wondered, before it transferred to the car itself, and my passengers? Before long, it could be running rampage across the whole of Norfolk, Britain, the world. How, I wondered, could it ever be eradicated? The only way, perhaps, would be by bringing an even bigger, more putrid smell to suffocate it.

Dave was taking his time coming to collect the horse

skulls, and I hadn't actually had any reason to venture into the cockpit since I'd first put them there. The way I looked at it was that they were horse skulls, and I had no reason to go and check to see that they were still horse skulls. On the day I finally ventured into the room, I was on my way to retrieve a beanbag to provide extra seating for some friends I had staying over that night. This was a beanbag I tended to keep out of the way, as it had a habit of leaking beans, which Janet would then get stuck to his tail, and spread around the house to unexpectedly devastating effect. I did slightly wonder if it was worth retrieving it, as there was always the possibility that, having smelled The Smell, my friends wouldn't even get to the point of taking a seat. However, this proved to be a moot dilemma, as what hit me when I opened the cockpit door made it impossible to venture to the other side of the room to get the beanbag in question.

An old neighbour of mine, Mary, had an expression that I am rather fond of which she used to describe bad smells. 'Ooh, it really meets ya!' she used to say. But the odour in the cockpit didn't just meet me; it enclosed me in a bear hug like some needy psychopath. Covering my face with a tea towel, I inched across the room, then dragged the thick polythene bags containing the skulls outside onto the balcony. I then ran to the bathroom and washed my hands approximately seven times in a row. I also had a vague, inexplicable instinct to clean my teeth. I wouldn't be so presumptuous to specu-late that this was what it might feel like to be personally violated, but I definitely had never before experienced a sense of invasion: had I been felt up by a member of the undead, I imagined I would have had a similar reaction.

The horse skulls had left a small stain in the cockpit, in the shape of a smaller horse skull. I preferred not to speculate as regards the stain's contents, but whatever it was, it had leaked through a thick bag, and proved largely resistant to my attempts to scrub it out of the parquet flooring. Even with the skulls outside, and the help of a slightly industrial cleaning session, the smell lingered for a few more days. Its dominance had been such that I almost expected it to infiltrate the outside of the house as well, leading to complaints from neighbours, but the skulls became a more benign presence after that. As I passed them on my travels, I began to think of them quite fondly, and named them Ned and Ed. I felt a little sorry for them sitting out there, unloved, although I stopped short of Dee's suggestion of bringing them back in, putting pot pourri in their brain cavities, and using them as an elaborate pair of bookends.

The bags containing the skulls were tied now, as a feline-related precaution, but, because the bags were transparent, I could see their faces. Ned was an easygoing type, pretty much happy with his lot in life as long as he maintained his lake view and continued to be able to feel the morning sun on his bones, but Ed had just a slight sarcastic smirk about him with which I wasn't quite comfortable. As I watered the plants or put fresh nuts out for visiting birdlife, I could feel his look. 'So,' he seemed to be saying. 'When's it going to happen? You've been wriggling out of it for a while now, haven't you, but you can't put it off forever.'

It was true: it had been a long time since I'd ridden a horse, and there was nobody to blame for this but me. The one time I'd finally looked like committing to my first ride off the rope, with Karl, Naomi, Steve, Sue and Dee, when I'd first met the recalcitrant Boris, Leo had been my saviour.

But I could only go on promising and not delivering for so long, and one day, in the autumn of 2007, a few days before Dave collected Ned and Ed, I ventured out onto the balcony, saw both of them looking a little forlorn, and made a decision.

'Okay,' I told Ned. 'You've convinced me.'

'I'm glad you've seen sense,' said Ed. 'I mean: look at the two of us. Do you really think we could do much to harm you?'

'So,' I said to Dee that night. 'Fancy a ride this weekend?'

We chose the same stable, near the village of Wilsham, where I'd been granted a get out of jail card before. We knew the route was a beautiful one, passing commons, heath land, and a succession of pretty Georgian houses and walled gardens, all of which were that much easier to admire from an elevated position. We also knew that the stables were overseen by a riding instructor called Carol, who Dee assured me was a calming person to be riding with. We chose the same time of day as the last ride: about an hour and a half before dusk, when the falling sun would render the fields crisp and golden.

On the afternoon we arrived, I was feeling queasy. My stomach was bad, and an old back problem had recurred, sending my lower vertebrae into minor spasms. But when I alluded to this to Dee, I could see the disappointment in her eyes, and I knew that I had already used up my wimping out credits. Also, if I went for the cowardly option, I would be wasting the thirty-pounds fee for the second time in a row. I resolved to stay committed to the day's mission, and somehow kept this resolve when a never-more obstinate Boris was brought out and placed in front of me like some blackly comic offering from the Dark Gods of Hoof. The resolve also stayed when I realised we would be supervised on the ride not by Carol, but by two stable hands: a dark-haired, sullen girl of about fourteen, and a lanky, blond, constantly chewing boy of about sixteen, or what I might have described behind their backs as 'two tiny children'.

It would be easy to compare riding a horse for the first time off the rope to riding a bike for the first time without stabilisers. It would also be inaccurate. A bike does not like to munch leaves, nor is it capable of freaking out and crushing your brain, rendering you a vegetable who needs to spend the rest of his life being transported around in a wheelbarrow by a benevolent friend. Boris was actually quite well behaved for the first half mile, but I could tell he could sense my physical discomfort and the extra position of weakness this would put me in. I remembered seeing the difficulty Steve had had riding him all those months ago: the way he chuntered and scraped his foot and refused to stay with the main party.

I looked to the teenagers for reassurance, but they were off in their own world, discussing their friends' recent Facebook status updates. Apparently, Sadie had been vague-booking[5] again, only saying that she was well pissed off with *someone* but not who it was but everyone knew it was Mark, because he'd been cheating on her with that slag from Somerfield again, even though she had her tongue pierced and only, like, last week he was sitting in Starbucks in front of *everyone* going 'I would, like, *never* do it with a girl with any piercings apart from in her ear'. This revelation was far

---

[5] A deliberately vague Facebook status, often serving as a cry for help, or attention, and prompting your friends to ask you what is up: e.g. 'Sadie is so fed up with *some* people'.

more interesting than the safety concerns of two thirty-something horse tourists, and I have to confess I was slightly disappointed not to catch the end of the story myself, as Boris and I dropped behind the other three horses, Boris finding a selection of fascinating grasses, leaves and branches to busy himself with.

'Are you okay back there, Tom?' asked Dee.

'Er, yep! Fine,' I lied, pulling on Boris's reins to little effect.

We'd come off the bridleway and onto a road, but Boris insisted on walking at the top of the steep grass verge, making for a bouncy ride. I was already sizing up my leap into the abyss, making little practice movements with my legs, wondering how easy it would be to prevent getting one of them caught in the stirrups and get dragged along behind Boris, upside down, like some slightly less masculine version of Calamity Jane. I would have voiced my worries to the teenagers, but I could already hear in my head how pathetic it would sound: the pleading of a child to other children.

Hundreds of years ago, men of my age and physique were supposed to ride horses as a matter of routine. The only time they would have had a genuine concern about falling off was when somebody was shooting bullets or arrows at them. Weren't these brave, unreconstructed males the kind I aspired to be, deep down? I needed to take control – that was what I'd been told to do, wasn't it? But the funny thing was, when Boris bolted, he did so at the exact point I'd made the decision to man up and take control of the situation. I have no idea what caused it – perhaps he'd eaten a bad leaf, or suddenly felt insecure about being away from the gelding that Dee was riding – but I took it as a direct, stubborn response to what I was thinking.

In times to come, I'll probably remember Boris's run as being considerably longer. Time will no doubt colour and exaggerate it. Maybe I'll add a couple of jumped hedges and some nightmare whinnying, a flashing vision of my own corpse, a startled farmer opening his mouth and dropping the piece of straw he'd been chewing as we flew past him. In truth, it probably lasted about forty seconds, but that was long enough for Boris to go up and down the bank at the side of the road, and charge past his fellow horses.

I'm not certain where the dividing line is drawn between jumping from a horse and being thrown, but I sense I was only just one side of it, though I'm not quite sure which side. In future, I imagine it will depend on my mood: if I'm with someone I want to impress, I'll say I was thrown. If I'm feeling humble, I'll probably say I jumped. Whatever the case, and whoever instigated it, my parting of ways from Boris was well timed. I came easily out of the stirrups, and I landed on my side, not my aching back. The one drawback was that the surface I landed on happened to be tarmac, not grass.

'It was pretty amazing,' Dee would later remember. 'You did a sort of commando roll.'

She was probably being generous, but I'd certainly contorted my body in some impact-softening manner. Picking myself up, I realised I was reasonably unhurt. My hip ached, and, rolling up my trouser leg, I saw that I'd scraped a lengthy strip of skin off my shin, but I could walk. For a seventeenth-century cavalier, this was the equivalent of a paper cut. At the same time, though, I didn't much feel like falling off Boris again, and expressed as much to the other three riders.

'Oh, he won't do it again,' said the boy teenager, who seemed rather frustrated with my antics. 'He'll be *fine*.' But how, I wondered, could he be so sure? Did Boris have a special reputation for throwing his riders off once as a 'test' then warming to them? I doubted it.

'It's entirely up to you,' said Dee.

I could see from her look – slightly more gentle than the one she usually used when we were discussing horses – that she knew I was at a crossroads. I loved golf as much as she loved horses. She'd given the sport a go at the local driving range, and decided it wasn't for her, and that was fine. But there'd never been a make or break moment there, not like this.

They say that the only thing to do when you fall off a horse is to get straight back on. If I didn't, I might never ride again. I could live with that, if Dee could too.

As I announced my decision, the natural world seemed to rise up around me. Everyone in the vicinity was looking down at me. Dee. The sulky teenager. The chewing teenager. The three teenagers they were on top of. And the most teenage teenager of all: Boris. The blond stable hand had caught up with him and got him on the rope again now, and, suitably chastised, he looked happier. As he and the others trotted away without me, I was surprised not to feel like a failure. Instead, I just felt a sensation of overwhelming, peaceful smallness: a pleasant one that would stay with me for the duration of the long, lonely walk back to the stable, and was not undermined by the realisation that, during my decision-making process, I'd been standing in some of Boris's freshly deposited manure.

How to Medicate an Intellectually Challenged Cat: Instructions for Housesitters

1. Clear space on kitchen work surface. Scan surface for sharp or burning objects, keeping in mind The Time Intellectually Challenged Fluffy Cat Resembling Rock Musician Pete Townshend Set Fire To His Tail By Walking Too Close To A Candle. Arrange food dishes and remove two pills from jar priced erroneously and unfairly excitingly on Internet at '50p for 30!' (actual price: 50p each).
2. Call cats, using special patented Tomwhistle.
3. Place pouches of meaty slop on kitchen counter, carefully avoiding three-year-old packets of Felix As Good as it Looks (aka As Bad as it Smells) at rear of food drawer. Dispense meaty slop.
4. Throw Intellectually Challenged Cat Resembling TV

Food Enthusiast Hugh Fearnley-Whittingstall off kitchen counter with one hand, while using other hand to carefully place two pink pills inside one dish of meaty slop. If possible, try to insert pills into meaty chunks themselves, rather than just into jelly. While doing this, try not to dwell overly on substance concerned. Think of it this way: yes, it smells, but if you really thought about an egg or some milk, you probably wouldn't want to go near that either.

5. Wash hands, thoroughly.

6. Dive across kitchen, just in time to remove face of Intellectually Challenged Cat Resembling TV Food Enthusiast Hugh Fearnley-Whittingstall from pilled dish of meaty slop.

7. While looking the other way and pretending to be occupied, quickly swoop down and pick up Intellectually Challenged Fluffy Cat Resembling Rock Musician Pete Townshend. Pick up pilled dish of meaty slop, and place cat and slop in adjacent room.

8. Remove face of Intellectually Challenged Cat Resembling TV Food Enthusiast Hugh Fearnley-Whittingstall from bottom of Intellectually Challenged Fluffy Cat Resembling Rock Musician Pete Townshend, and close door, firmly.

9. Feed remaining five cats. For full instructions on feeding, refer to 'How to Feed Six Sodding Cats: Instructions for Housesitters' (*Under the Paw*, Simon & Schuster, 2008).

10. Open door of adjacent room, and release Intellectually Challenged Fluffy Cat Resembling Rock Musician Pete Townshend back into kitchen. Collect leftover pills from Intellectually Challenged Fluffy Cat Resembling

Rock Musician Pete Townshend's now otherwise empty bowl, and place on kitchen counter.

11. Chase Intellectually Challenged Fluffy Cat Resembling Rock Musician Pete Townshend downstairs, maintaining enough speed not to lose sight of Intellectually Challenged Fluffy Cat Resembling Rock Musician Pete Townshend, but not so much speed that Intellectually Challenged Fluffy Cat Resembling Rock Musician Pete Townshend runs out of cat flap in fear.

12. Carefully circle Intellectually Challenged Fluffy Cat Resembling Rock Musician Pete Townshend, feigning great interest in object in entirely opposite direction from Intellectually Challenged Fluffy Cat Resembling Rock Musician Pete Townshend.

13. At the count of three (please note: counting should be done purely in own head), dive at Intellectually Challenged Fluffy Cat Resembling Rock Musician Pete Townshend.

14. Pick self up off floor, ignoring disdainful looks of suddenly appearing Sensitive Artistic Secret Warlord Cat. Sit down in Formerly Sumptuously Restored 1970s Armchair Now Permanently Jealously Overseen By Attention Seeking Grey Dwarf Cat. Relax and clear mind of feline-related thoughts, being sure to avail self of film collection on adjacent shelf. Please note: for purposes of continued mind-clearing, best to avoid *The Complete Bagpuss* DVD.

15. Wait ten minutes, then return upstairs. Call cats, using special patented Tomwhistle.

16. Throw Intellectually Challenged Cat Resembling TV Food Enthusiast Hugh Fearnley-Whittingstall off kitchen counter.

17. Gingerly creep downstairs, gently calling Intellectually Challenged Fluffy Cat Resembling Rock Musician Pete Townshend.

18. Pick Intellectually Challenged Fluffy Cat Resembling Rock Musician Pete Townshend's claw out of back, having not realised that, while you were heading downstairs, looking for Intellectually Challenged Fluffy Cat Resembling Rock Musician Pete Townshend, Intellectually Challenged Fluffy Cat Resembling Rock Musician Pete Townshend was above you, playing a game of 'Prison' (aka 'Use Bars Of Balustrade As Protection While Violently Batting Soft Parts Of Passing Unsuspecting Humans').

19. Open fridge, and retrieve Tesco Finest Honey Roast Ham from special minus-one-degree compartment in fridge. Place on kitchen counter.

20. Open cat food drawer, and keep Intellectually Challenged Fluffy Cat Resembling Rock Musician Pete Townshend's interest by rustling sachet of meaty slop.

21. Take Tesco Finest Honey Roast Ham to pills. Realise 'pills' is now in fact 'pill'.

22. Pick up Intellectually Challenged Cat Resembling TV Food Enthusiast Hugh Fearnley-Whittingstall and notice telltale pink smear around mouth of Intellectually Challenged Cat Resembling TV Food Enthusiast Hugh Fearnley-Whittingstall.

23. Wash hands, thoroughly.

24. Secrete remaining pill inside sheet of Tesco Finest Honey Roast Ham, creating pill sandwich. Step boldly towards Intellectually Challenged Fluffy Cat Resembling Rock Musician Pete Townshend and sweep Intellectually Challenged Fluffy Cat Resembling Rock Musician Pete

Townshend off floor, then feed pill sandwich to Intellectually Challenged Fluffy Cat Resembling Rock Musician Pete Townshend.

25. Witness small, girlish meow, and realise that, in attempting to follow 'How to Feed Six Sodding Cats' instructions, one cat, Prettyboy Tabby Cat, was omitted from melee.

26. Place Prettyboy Tabby Cat on Strange Plastic Grandma Stool, with dish of meaty slop.

27. Watch Intellectually Challenged Fluffy Cat Resembling Rock Musician Pete Townshend begin to convulse in corner of room.

28. Grab kitchen roll and dive, belatedly, in direction of Intellectually Challenged Fluffy Cat Resembling Rock Musician Pete Townshend.

29. Cautiously examine effluence of Intellectually Challenged Fluffy Cat Resembling Rock Musician Pete Townshend, finding no pink pill.

30. Double-bag effluence of Intellectually Challenged Fluffy Cat Resembling Rock Musician Pete Townshend and place in dustbin.

31. Sigh, and wash hands, thoroughly. Spot pink pill – now quarter of former size – stuck to trouser leg.

32. Repair to fridge, retrieve butter, and firmly cut off thumb-sized knob. Place pill inside knob.

33. Repair to bathroom, and grab clean towel from rack.

34. Sweep Intellectually Challenged Fluffy Cat Resembling Rock Musician Pete Townshend off floor, harshly curtailing second game of 'Prison' in ten minutes, and swaddle Intellectually Challenged Fluffy Cat Resembling Rock Musician Pete Townshend in towel.

35. Insert buttered pill between Intellectually Challenged

Fluffy Cat Resembling Rock Musician Pete Townshend's mouth, and gently but firmly clamp shut.

36. Wait ninety seconds, gently rubbing throat of Intellectually Challenged Fluffy Cat Resembling Rock Musician Pete Townshend.

37. Watch as pink and yellow liquid oozes from mouth of Intellectually Challenged Fluffy Cat Resembling Rock Musician Pete Townshend.

38. Place Intellectually Challenged Fluffy Cat Resembling Rock Musician Pete Townshend on floor.

39. Open fridge, retrieving remainder of Tesco Finest Honey Roast Ham, chicken curry leftovers, spare ribs and kabano sausages (six pack). Open all packaging, and place on floor.

40. Pick up coat and bag. Wipe hands on corduroy jacket belonging to male owner of Intellectually Challenged Fluffy Cat Resembling Rock Musician Pete Townshend.

41. Exit house, posting spare keys through letterbox.

42. Receive phone call from owners of Intellectually Challenged Fluffy Cat Resembling Rock Musician Pete Townshend. Answer in high-pitched voice of elderly lady called Joan, from Fife, and profess ignorance of any subject mentioned. When subject of cats comes up, begin to talk about son's upcoming rowing final. Please note: if actually called Joan, elderly, with rowing champion son, and from Fife in real life, choose different identity.

43. Call phone company and request new numbers.

44. Write note to self on hand: 'Locksmith?'

45. Pour large glass of wine, and run bath.

46. Rummage in bottom of bag, and find bath bomb, bought from popular natural cosmetic company and summarily forgotten about two weeks previously.

47. Gently crumble and add bath bomb to warm, flowing water, savouring aroma.
48. Light candle.
49. Relax into suds, feeling physically and spiritually cleansed, and looking boldly towards future.

Remember You're a Womble

It is quite possible that, during the 1980s, there was not another man in Britain more worried about the possibility of his house exploding than my dad. Setting off from Nottinghamshire for our annual summer holiday, the routine would always be the same. We'd be about ten miles down the M1, the car weighed down with camping gear and back issues of the *Beano*, when he would turn to my mum, worry etched across his face. 'AH SAY, WE DID SWITCH THE HOB OFF, JO, DIDN'T WE?' he'd ask.

My mum would do her best to offer reassurance, but her response would essentially be immaterial. Sometimes we'd manage to get as far as Leicester Forest East service station while the two of them tried to convince themselves that flames were not licking their way malevolently up their woodchip, but with my dad's question, the seed of doubt had been irrevocably planted, and we would eventually, inevitably, turn back. Upon arriving home, of course, my parents would find that the hob was not on at all, though this would not prevent the following thing happening next year, and the year after that (the purchase

of a family coffee machine in 1993 only complicated matters further).

I used to sigh at such neurotic behaviour back then, but
the older I get, the worse I find I get at leaving the house.
The main difference is that when I return through the front
door to check that I haven't, for some unfathomable reason,
suddenly, without noticing, developed a penchant for can-
dles and left one burning in the living room, I am not
worrying primarily about losing my material possessions; I
am worrying about losing my cats.

I would like to think that, were my house to begin to fill
with smoke, the furry degenerates I live with would have the
wherewithal to quickly get out of one of their two cat flaps,
but how can I know that for certain? A couple of them
aren't even bright enough to remember to put their tongues
back in their mouths after they've finished licking themselves. Others can't get through a day without getting one of
their legs trapped in their collar, flicking one of those cat
flaps into a permanently locked position, or scalding themselves by experimentally placing their front paws on an
electric heater. Do these animals really sound wily enough
to distinguish 'everyday warmth' from 'potentially life-
threatening blaze'? And what if it happened to be snowing
when the house caught fire? Faced with the choice between
that horrible cold white stuff and the gentle, sparky simmer
of an overfed multi-socket adaptor, I sense that the decision
would be a no-brainer, in more ways than one.

Just before Christmas 2008, I read a news report about six
Buckinghamshire felines being revived after a house fire. It
was simultaneously sad and uplifting, and resulted in one of
the sweetest cat photographs of the year, depicting a fireman
fitting a ginger and white moggy with a baby-sized oxygen

mask. However, it also suggested that the first instinct of a cat, when faced with a room full of smoke, might not be to evacuate the premises, but simply to hide.

It's not just the image of a neglected flame that lights the touchpaper of my travelling imagination. Often, having already returned to the house once to confirm that Pablo or Janet have not accidentally switched the gas hob on with their tails, I've been known to unlock the door one more time, just on the off chance that, while going about my daily business, I have left the sink running, with the plug in, and a live socket has been clandestinely fitted next to it without my knowledge.

When Dee and I went on a rare holiday, to Somerset, in 2007, it was not a conflagration that I became convinced we had left behind us, but a forlorn Bootsy, trapped behind the radiator cover in the entrance hall. On one hand, this was a perfectly valid concern: Bootsy, being so minuscule, had a habit at that point of somehow slithering underneath the wooden radiator cover in question, then not being able to get out, and the entrance hall was the hottest room in the house by some distance – especially in June.

On the other hand, it was absurd to imagine that, even if Bootsy had ventured into the entrance hall, she'd not scampered back into the main part of the house as I loaded the back seat of the car with heavy bags, and traffic whizzed by on the road beyond. Even if she had got stuck, it was also hard to picture a scene in which a cat as vocal as her would not let us know at the earliest opportunity, but I somehow managed to conjure up the necessary imaginative powers to do so. From the moment we left the M25, I drove Dee towards Swindon, and also towards distraction, by repeatedly replaying my final moves in leaving the house, until I became convinced that at that very moment Bootsy's tiny, grey, dehydrated form was croaking fruitlessly for help. Had we not happened to be paying a lady called Sarah to do some garden maintenance for us on the day in question, and been able to telephone her to ask her to look through the letterbox and confirm the entrance hall was feline-free, I have no doubt that I would have turned the car around and added another four hundred miles to our trip with little compunction.

I have not really had a break long enough to merit the word 'holiday' since then. On top of my reluctance to ask friends or neighbours to feed my cats and my belief that if I put my cats in a cattery they would hold a grudge against me forever, there is an additional problem: in early 2009, Janet was diagnosed with an overactive thyroid gland.

I've tried various methods of administering the two small pink pills that Janet must be given to keep his thyroid steady. These have included The Towel Wrap, The Throat Rub, The Pâté Treat, and The Pea Shooter. Perhaps the most successful method has been burying the pills in the trays of terrine-style cat food that can be found in some shops. This is not infallible, though. And while I have some very good friends I feel I can count on in times of trouble, I have to ask myself the question: can you ever really know a person well enough to ask them to spend a week dipping their fingers inside mechanically recovered meat?

The Bear and Janet are now officially old cats, but their aging processes have varied markedly. When I first met The Bear, he was already a wizened survivor, an ornery old gentleman of strange, powerful dignity. If he vanished for a few days, you could guarantee he would return with some new ailment or battle scar. Yet, since then, he has become visibly younger.

Certainly, his walk does not speak of youthful vigour: it's the paranoid scuttle of a cat who believes he has a hell-hound – or at least a bored Shipley – on his tail. But his face and demeanour actually seem to be making a bid for the youth he never quite had. His eyes have always looked directly at me in a manner matched by no other cat, but their stare has got brighter, and his fur – at least in the period when he's not due another jab for his flea allergy – correspondingly plusher. He's sometimes mistaken for Shipley – no doubt much to his chagrin – by those who don't know him well, but his features are far more exotic: strangely fox-like, but also unignorably evocative of the word 'snufflepig'.

At fifteen, The Bear has still never, to the best of my knowledge, killed another living creature, but he's become more playful than ever. When he bats and chews one of his many extra-strength catnip cigars, he takes periodic, nervous looks over his shoulder, as if aware that what he is doing is fundamentally beneath him, and keen that other, intellectually inferior cats do not catch him indulging in such lowbrow pursuits. He still mostly keeps himself to himself, and knows all the best hiding places, but is newly prone to isolated moments of exhibitionism. Not long after I purchased the cats a new toy on which to sharpen their claws, the overexcitably named Kitty Boutique Disco Pole, I found him perched, with perfect balance, on top of the central podium: his own version of the Fourth Plinth, a place above all the riff-raff where he could cogitate over the meaning of life. When guests are over at the house, he will emerge more frequently than he once might have, and walk determinedly, with his signature wobble, towards the most intense or melancholic of them, his eyes never leaving theirs.

Old age has also brought a love interest for The Bear, in

the form of Biscuit, the aging, plump ginger lady cat that lives next door. I'm assured by my neighbours, Deborah and David, that their *Last of the Summer Wine* romance does not extend much further than over-the-fence chats, longing looks through Deborah and David's kitchen window (The Bear's) and flirtatiously grumpy rebukes (Biscuit's), but after a couple of years, the flame shows no sign of blowing out.

This is all in sharp contrast to Janet, who, in his youth, was always a hulking good-time cat, but, by 2008, had become more prone to crotchety eccentricities, and was visibly fading as a physical specimen. Right from the moment that the young Shipley had first set eyes on him, the two of them had always made time for at least one wrestle per day. This was strictly play fighting, in which Janet's supremacy was challenged but never quite questioned, a far different contact sport to Ralph's tussles with Pablo. Occasionally, heads bounced against furniture and chunks of fur flew, but nobody ended up growling and hissing in a corner. But now when Shipley instigated an encounter, I noticed Janet slinking away, flustered, and retreating behind a chair or table, where he could be found panting nervously. Simultaneously, his appetite became greater, and his habit of tripping me up on the stairs or batting me through the bars of the balustrade more frequent. He had long been perfecting a special 'fart hiss' during times of trouble. In the past this had caused confusion as to its point of origin, but as it became more vehement and heartfelt, there was no doubt which orifice it was emerging from.

During a routine examination in May that year, the vet held a stethoscope to Janet's chest and looked up at me gravely.

'I'm afraid she has a heart murmur,' he said.

I opened my mouth to do what I always do when I take Janet to the vet, which is explain exactly why he's not a she – a story which usually involves a shrug and the use of the phrase 'it's very fluffy down there' – but thought better of it. Instead I asked, 'So what exactly does that mean?'

'Well, it doesn't mean too much right now,' said the vet. 'We use a scale of one to six to measure the intensity of the murmur, and she's a three, which means she's not in need of medication at this point. Do you ever notice her panting?'

'Yes, quite often.'

'The important thing is to keep her away from activities that get her overexcited.'

After packing Janet back into his extra-large cat basket and enduring a couple of particularly fervent fart-hisses, I began to ponder the vet's advice. Precisely what activities *did* get Janet overexcited? And how would I keep him away from them? It wasn't as if I could sit him down quietly and break it to him that the time had come in his life to give up his pentathlon ambitions and stay away from Norfolk's many tempting topless bars. Much of his energetic life took place far away from me, in an unknown nocturnal world. The best I felt I could do in the circumstances was intercede when Shipley made a beeline for him and keep him away from uncut catnip. I also began to feed him in a separate area to the other cats. Yet no amount of food seemed to satisfy Janet. He always seemed skittish, weaving around my legs asking for more, asking for something, but not, evidently, affection.

In addition to constant hunger, Janet's illness manifested itself in another, more unexpected way, too: tidying.

∵

As anybody who owns them knows, cats are remarkably clean animals. This is because they are uniquely skilled in wiping the dirty parts of themselves on other things and people. Possessing a particular talent for this is Janet, who, after a journey outside, will leave approximately a third of his loose unwanted body mass on the carpet and duvet cover. He's always been a thorough groomer, but after he became ill, his cleaning sessions gained a new intensity. The vet told me that this was a symptom of stress. I'm not sure, however, that you could put his new, rather curious style of extracurricular cleaning down to the same thing.

Because of the structure of my house, the fence to the front of it, and the gradient of the hill it's built into, my garden is not easily accessible to intruders. The place, however, has always been a magnet for litter. On those Wild West Friday nights in which East Mendleham specialises, bottles and chip trays fly over the fence and catch in the hilly, loamy beds to the right of the house. Meanwhile, old crisp packets, bottles and cans often wash up on the shore of the lake at the bottom of the garden. These are the danger spots, and, apart from that, the rest of the garden is usually pretty clean. But for the last few weeks, I'd noticed a new, creeping spread to the litter, into the main part of the garden, directly behind the building.

When Dee and I first bought the house, it had been only part-occupied for the preceding months, and we found chewing gum, condom wrappers and cigarette butts on the patio – a sure sign that kids had been using it as a venue for multi-purpose lurking. It seemed unlikely that the culprits had mysteriously returned after four and a half years – they would probably have grown out of such pursuits, having almost started primary school by now – but it seemed equally unlikely that the wind had blown quite this much litter to the direct rear of the house. It started to occur to me that the only reason for finding five empty packets of Spicy Tomato Wheat Crunchies on your flagstones was that some-one had been sitting on your flagstones, eating five packets of Spicy Tomato Wheat Crunchies.

I tried to stay vigilant, keeping my eyes and ears open, even contemplating creeping downstairs in the middle of the night and bursting abruptly out the back door and shouting 'CAUGHT YOU!' but to no avail. The litter con-tinued to accumulate, in the area directly behind the back door and my study window, with no obvious source. Before long, disposing of soggy Mr Kipling packets and crinkled, greying Sunblest bags became no less an intrinsic part of my morning ritual than making coffee, turning the kitchen tap to a trickle to meet Bootsy's demanding thirst-related needs and shouting at the presenters of BBC Breakfast for speaking to me as if I was simple.

What was almost as spooky as the appearance of the litter was its frequent vintage. I'm aware that there are some fairly timeworn products knocking around East Mendleham – one of its kebab shops had only recently got rid of the last of a supply of bright red ring-pull Coke cans that I'd suspected were 'retro' in a worryingly genuine way – but many of the brands residing in my flowerbed hadn't been widely available in supermarkets since the last Conservative gov-ernment. 'Do people still really eat Mini Gems?' I found myself asking. The following weekend, I even found some Bird's Instant Whip, a product with which I hadn't come into contact since my mum flicked some of it at my dad and my Uncle Tony on a family camping trip in 1984.

Of course, I'd seen Janet lazing about next to the rubbish

as it appeared, but it didn't initially occur to me to connect the pile of litter with the pile of cat alongside it. Janet, who's more of a dozer than a sleeper, can do his lazing in a remarkably eclectic array of habitats, and his penchant for hard surfaces was one of the quirks of his middle-age, alongside his ever-loudening yawn and that increasingly ubiquitous fart-hiss. If he was lying on the flagstones, next to a faded box that once contained some Findus Crispy Pancakes, was that really such odd behaviour for an eleven-year-old cat debilitated by a heart murmur and an IQ of twelve? Maybe not. I did, however, start to have my suspicions when one day I found him loitering just outside the back door, meowing mournfully, with a full, sealed bag of pre-Gary Lineker era Walkers Salt & Vinegar sitting a matter of millimetres from him on the ground. These suspicions were confirmed during one of the final days of summer 2008, with the help of Deborah next door.

For some reason known only to them, it delights my cats when I go out into the garden. If the weather is balmy, and it's been a day or two since I've ventured out, it will take a matter of seconds before each of them emerge onto the lawn alongside me. It's as if they are celebrating me coming to my senses and realising that true life is not spent in front of a TV, cooker or computer, but in the undergrowth, rooting out voles and marking the pampas grass with the most quintessential scent I can muster. Shipley is particularly hyperactive in this situation, and will usually hurtle down the steep lawn behind me, building the momentum needed to shin up his favourite apple tree at the bottom of the slope. As a single, continuous, fifty-yard move ending at the summit of the second-highest tree in the garden, it's impressive, but perhaps not quite as much so as Shipley believes, and I will often puncture his self-delight by heading straight back towards the house. At this point he will chase me back up the lawn, clapping the back of my legs in outrage.

I'm sure all this looks very odd to normal people, such as the taciturn gardener who'd done some clearance for Dee and me earlier in 2008: one of those slow-moving, brusque, dog-owning, inexpressive fiftysomething men who seem to live in every third cottage in Norfolk. No doubt Phil from Get Yer Phil Garden Maintenance was bemused to find a small, demanding, grey she-cat repeatedly hurling herself in front of his feet as he walked up the lawn, while her owner collected wet, crumpled packets of Salted Chipsticks from the undergrowth, while getting his calves clawed by a bigger, black male cat who appeared to swear, rather than meow. Phil remained cool in the face of Bootsy's flirtation, but I liked to think I could see the mental battle going on behind his eyes: one part of him screaming 'Go on! Stroke her! You know you want to!' while the other countered with 'No! Don't be so preposterous! You are a man approaching sixty with a German shepherd and an extensive collection of trowels! Think what this would do to your reputation!' I decided then was not the time to warn him about the demanding frenzy Shipley will go into any time he spots a man wearing gardening gloves, an item of outdoor wear which he perceives as a slightly dirtier, but no less enjoyable, alternative to his favourite pet mitt.

Having lived next door to me for a number of years, Deborah is far more accustomed to observing this kind of chaos, but I was still a little embarrassed to see her emerge from behind the hedge and spot me holding in one hand a soggy Golden Virginia packet and a water-filled bag formerly hosting some Merry Maid chocolate caramels, and on the other a gardening glove, with which I was massaging Shipley's scruff, to his beatific delight. We greeted each other in the usual way: her asking after the cats' health, a brief update on the unrequited love between The Bear and Biscuit, and my usual apologies for the numerous occasions recently when Ralph had sat in a bush in her garden and howled his own name at the top of his voice.

'More litter, then?' she said, acknowledging the contents of my left hand. 'It's amazing what he does with it. I've never seen a cat do that before.'

'Who? Do what?'

'Who? Janet, of course! Who else? I see him fishing it out of the lake and walking up your garden with it between his teeth. He brought some up to my back door the other day. An old packet of fisherman's bait, I think.'

With the possible exception of Pablo, Janet had, over the years, been arguably the least enigmatic of my cats. He'd never really had much time for gammon or smoked salmon or even the more expensive cat food Dee and I sometimes purchased for The Bear. Maybe it was because he originally hailed from the East End of London, but he liked his meat as jellified as possible, with no frills. Had he been one of my male friends, on a night out, he would have been the kind who insisted on finishing up in a kebab shop, and would make a point of getting on first-name terms with the owner, in hope of future discounts. His life as a predator, meanwhile, was simple and uncompetitive compared to his feline housemates. Essentially, put him in an evenly matched tussle on the kitchen floor with half a Savoy cabbage, and he was happy.

Unlike The Bear or Bootsy, Janet never gave me the sense that he was plotting to take over the world, and, unlike Shipley and Ralph, he never gave me the sense that he was plotting to take over me, but, like all cats, he had his mysteries, even if they were slightly vacant ones. His love of litter was the biggest and most vacant yet. Without doubt, I was grateful that he was saving me making my weekly trip to the lakeside to collect the detritus from the shore, but was being helpful really his intention? Was a crumpled, squashed can of Lilt just a 'present': his pacifist's version of the shrews and voles Shipley, Ralph and Pablo left outside the bedroom door? I felt it was more than that: that he was looking to find some cure for his ills in the depths of his garbage.

In her later years, my parents' last cat, Daisy, had suffered from an overactive thyroid gland. Admittedly, when her thyroid problems began, Daisy had never looked for solace in three-year-old Blackcurrant Flavour Ice Snappers or Original Pom-Bears: The Teddy-Shaped Potato Snack, but I was familiar with some of the other symptoms of the disease, so when I took Janet to the vet, concerned about his further weight loss, I wasn't surprised to hear my fears confirmed. Dee and I were left with two choices to treat Janet's hyperthyroidism: a daily course of tablets, or an expensive radiation procedure in which Janet would be sent away for several weeks to have the tumour in his thyroid gland shrunk.

We knew that committing to the former option would mean that there would never again be a time in Janet's life when he would not need medication, but we also were reluctant to choose the latter – not just because of the astro-nomical cost, but because it would mean sending a lonely, confused cat with a heart condition away from home for what to us would seem an agonisingly long period and what to him would probably seem an endless one.

The tablets were slow to take effect at first, and Janet ini-tially continued to lose weight. Way back when another vet had originally corrected Dee on his true gender, the vet had laughed, pointing out how unlikely it was that a cat so big could be female. In the past visitors had 'coo!'d and 'cor!'d over Janet's size. But now when I picked him up, he seemed more dishcloth than cat. If not for his impressive fluff, there would have been nothing to him.

Now that his hobby had been rumbled, he appeared to see no point in hiding his love of litter, and began to deposit it inside the house, with added sound effects. Bringing in, for example, a yellowing packet formerly containing some Wildlife Choobs jellybeans (Tagline: 'Baby Koalas are the size of a jellybean when they're born!'), he would announce his discovery with a mournful wail. It was the kind of noise you might imagine a cat making after it had waved its family off on holiday, only to see the miniature car they were driv-ing plunge over the side of a deep harbour.

I noticed that often, it seemed that the greener, older and more anonymous the litter, the louder the keening sound. To hear such a haunting wailing was baffling, but also somehow appropriate. Some of the cellophane bags he was bringing in were so old there seemed a genuine possi-bility they could contain their own resident spectre. Perhaps most worrying of all was the moment when I stumbled upstairs to make breakfast and almost stepped on a six-year-old used condom. Closer inspection, carried out with some rubber gloves, revealed it to be a more innocent item: a wet, cellophane tube of indeterminate – though almost certainly not carnal – heritage. However, I could not help but view it as a warning. I knew, from the mating calls I often heard from East Mendleham Park, that it was not impossible that the worst could one day happen: I might step sleepily past the cat flap one day, feel an unpleasant squelchy sensation, and realise I had a prophylactic attached to my big toe.

In the period Janet's illness had developed, there had been two major bird problems around the lake at the centre of East Mendleham. Firstly, for the previous eighteen months, the water had been infested with poisonous blue-green algae, decimating the local duck and goose population. Signs were posted on lampposts asking the public not to make the problem worse by throwing bread into the water, and even the old man who swore while throwing Hovis at the ducks had toned down his act somewhat.

Admittedly, the second bird problem was one that didn't impact on quite so much of the locality, but to my cats, it was no less critical. In recent weeks, an avian tormentor – I have no idea what kind of avian tormentor as it kept its identity top secret – had begun to imitate the whistle I used for my cats at mealtimes.

I already had a certain amount of experience with birds that mimicked the sounds of domestic life. A previous example of this was the Telephone Bird, which, for a couple of months, had sat outside the kitchen window, replicating the ring of the house's landline. Even more impressive, perhaps, was the Pablomeow Bird, whose cheep was a near-exact replica of the frenzied noise Pablo made at times of hunger.

The Foodwhistle Bird, however, was more sophisticated than its predecessors. Its taunts were not just designed to bamboozle but to seriously mess up a cat's diary.

My cats could probably just about distinguish between the noise I made and the noise the Foodwhistle Bird made, but it was a close call and, as it started its merry tune, Pablo and Janet could often be seen bolting through the cat flap into the kitchen, an eager look on their faces. Even at times of low-level hunger, their more unflappable peers, such as The Bear, could be seen opening one vaguely inquiring eye as it whistled. I was not sure if it was a mockingbird in any official sense, but even if it wasn't, it probably should have been made an honorary one. One thing was for sure: if at this point my cats were to co-author a book with the same title as a famous mid-twentieth-century novel written by Harper Lee, its theme would not be racial tension in the Deep South.

I had actually come across a nascent Foodwhistle Bird before, about fifteen years previously, while living with my parents, but this latest one was far more skilled at disorientating its victims. On one hand, I had to sit back and marvel at what an amazing evolutionary step it seemed to mark for mimicry. 'What could possibly come after the Foodwhistle Bird?' I wondered. 'The Really Hungry Tiger Bird? The Seinfeld Slap Bass Bird? The Jeremy Paxman Clearing His Throat On University Challenge Bird?' On the other hand, I decided to put my awe aside and take some action, for the good of my cats' sanity. After all, I'd been using the same whistle for the various cats in my life for three decades now, and perhaps the Foodwhistle Bird was a sign that it was time for a change.

I went over a few options. I could have experimented

with an entirely new whistle, but who's to say that, in time, that wouldn't have been appropriated by the Foodwhistle Bird as well? There was also the option of reverting to a roll call of names, but that seemed like needless extra work. Instead, I opted for my vinyl copy of 'My Sharona', the 1979 American number one hit by the power pop band The Knack. I'm not sure quite how the decision came about, other than one night at jellied meatslop-dispensing time I happened to be listening to it, and its jerky, near-spastic rhythms seemed appropriate to the manic process of feeding half a dozen furry forces of nature – particularly when Pablo mistimed a jump from the chair to the kitchen work surface and dive-bombed unceremoniously into a shelf of cookbooks.

In truth, I couldn't really tell if my cats could discern different types of music from one another. I had always felt that they had a particularly disapproving air about them when I was playing Hall and Oates' 'You Make My Dreams', but maybe that was largely a reaction to the special backwards dance I liked to do to it. Whatever the case, 'My Sharona', with its snappy riff, seemed as good an option as any for my experiment. Certainly better that than an eight-minute epic off the second Emerson Lake and Palmer album.

Within a week, results were visible. Usually, by the time The Knack had sung the opening refrain of 'Ooh my little pretty one', Bootsy and Pablo were weaving around my feet and by the point of the first 'my-my-my-my-Sharona' all six cats were filling their faces, but after two weeks I still couldn't tell if it was the new-wave guitars they were responding to or the clunking of food dishes. The experiment was still in its infancy, and had not yet proved to be an instant way of getting the cats' attention, so on the morning that Janet didn't turn up for his breakfast, I wasn't initially concerned. But because I'm a born worrier, knew how permanently hungry Janet was, and knew my cats had it too good these days to wander far from home, I eventually decided to stroll outside to see if I could locate him.

I found him lying flat on his stomach beneath the Cypress bush, a few yards from the back door. He had his chin pressed lethargically against the ground, and didn't even have the energy to wail at the empty Wotsit packet behind him. At my first touch, he fart-hissed, but it didn't have the passion of previous fart-hisses, giving the impression that, in fart-hiss terms, he was phoning it in somewhat. When I picked him up and carried him inside, I got the feeling he might have liked to have put up a fight, but didn't have the strength. He'd never felt lighter or more rag-like and, when I put him down, he slunk immediately behind the sofa.

Three hours later, with no sign of improvement, I helped hold him still on the examining table as the vet poked a thermometer up his bottom then filled him with antibiotics, professing an uncertainty as to what was the problem but saying that he was sure it wasn't connected with Janet's hyperthyroidism. Just four days previously, Janet had already been here for more blood tests, to determine whether he needed the dose of his hyperthyroid medication upped. That was not to mention my visit a week before that, when Shipley had scratched his retina and was forced to wear one of those lampshade-like collars. I was starting to wonder if, the next time I visited the surgery, it might be practical to pack not just my cats, but my toothbrush and pyjamas. I would be back again in three days for a progress check. All I could hope was that it was the same vet, so I didn't have to have the conversation about why Janet wasn't a girl for the third time in a week.

I had no idea whether cats could get blue-green algae poisoning. Considering the amount of stagnant water that had gone into Janet's mouth on his wombling trips of recent months, though, it probably shouldn't have been a surprise that he'd caught something nasty. But despite his already weak state, it *was* a surprise, and it floored me. For the next two days, no amount of meat, no matter how high or low quality, I waved in front of his face caught his interest. Old, slightly comical habits of his – his penchant for bringing twigs in on his tail, or the break-dance he did immediately before vomiting – now just seemed desperately sad.

There was another factor that was making Janet's demise even more difficult to watch: a few weeks earlier, in February 2009, Dee and I had split up. On one level, the two of us still laughed a lot together and had much in common. On another, deeper one, we'd become a small planet apart as people, wanted to do very different things with our time, and, after much deliberation, we'd realised that our relationship could not sustain this. We'd decided to live apart as a temporary measure, postponing thoughts of what might happen to the cats until a later date, but all the evidence pointed to the situation becoming permanent. For the moment, I was living alone in the house we'd shared, with the six cats that had been the crux of our life together, one of which was seriously ill.

You could say that, as Dee's ex-boyfriend's favourite cat, The Bear had cast his spell on the early months of our relationship, nine years earlier. But I'd never really felt The Bear was mine – or, rather, had felt he was even less mine than any other cat – in those days, and there had, initially, been some doubt whether he would live with us on a permanent basis. Janet, by contrast, was the first pet we'd shared: the cat that had brought me back to feline ownership after the one catless spell of my life. He'd been full of energy, shooting across the laminate floors of our first flat together in pursuit of ping-pong balls and catnip mice, his footfalls so heavy that the downstairs neighbour had requested that I walk around the place more quietly. Those feet were still heavy now, so much so that I would often hear him on the stairs and call out to Dee, mistaking him for her. Except what I was thinking of as 'now' wasn't 'now' at all: it was a few months before, when Janet still had enough meat on his bones to be heavy-footed, and there was still another person living here to mistake him for.

There is never a convenient time for a marriage to end, but it would have been doubly tragic if Janet's death marked the conclusion of my relationship with Dee. And even when, the morning before our return to the vet, I offered Janet a pouch of Sheba, and, very slowly, he slunk over and took a couple of tentative bites of it, I continued to dwell on an image that had been troubling me for weeks: of me with the other cats, alone, in the space where he and Dee used to be. I've never considered myself a morbid person, but I have to confess that I woke up more than once from a nightmare about me burying him, alone, in the garden. I was thirty-three, but was I really grown-up enough to cope with this? I suspected not.

These animals that shared our house were domestic only to their own ends, nobody's actual cats in spirit, but if they were anybody's, they were ours, not mine. Dee and I were still very much on speaking terms, and I kept her up to date with Janet's progress every day, but the point was: she wasn't here.

'He is twelve,' said Dee, ever the pragmatist. 'That's not a bad age for a cat.'

When people say, 'That's not a bad age for a cat', they don't mean that it's an age when a cat comes into his own, consolidates his finances, finally gets to drive the automobile that becomes him, and learns to be comfortable with his foibles; they mean the cat has done well to reach that age. I was surprised that Dee said it, but I also sensed she was distancing and protecting herself from the possibility that, at some point in the not too distant future, Janet might not be in her life at all. I also tried my best to see her point. Even now Janet was eating again, he was an underweight, nervous, unhappy cat with a heart condition and a tumour on his thyroid gland. On that evidence alone, it was best to be prepared for the worst. But was twelve really all that old? The Bear was fourteen and positively sashaying – albeit with a bit of a paranoid wiggle – into his prime.

In retrospect, performing a search on YouTube, in a tired and emotional state, for 'old cats' might not have been the best move. I came particularly close to being rendered to a globule of living blancmange by the moment in the home video of Cookie, a 26-year-old tabby from the American Midwest, shot a few months before her death, where the star looks up at the camera and lets out a croaky meow of such powerful abiding love, I feel faint just thinking about transcribing it. On the other hand, my virtual travels did lead me to Crème Puff, reportedly the oldest cat ever. Crème Puff lived with a man called Jake and, when she died in 2005, was thirty-eight years and three days old. If you'd spoken to Crème Puff not long before she left this mortal coil and she'd been able to speak, she would have been able to tell you about a world before the Manson family murders,

Led Zeppelin and the three-day week, a world when the JML pet mitt and the Happy Paws Bungalow were nothing more than the dreams of some crazy-haired feline-loving science fiction writer.

In the video, Jake, a man in his sixties in a baseball cap, took us around his Austin, Texas, shack, introducing us to his endless cats, which had names such as Red Dog and Jean Claude Van Damme. I especially liked the bit where he talked in his casual Texan way about having 'adopted over five hundred cats' over the years from his local shelter, as if he was talking about how many times he'd bought cigarettes from the 7-11 down the road. Jake attributed the longevity of so many of his cats to the bacon, eggs, broccoli and coffee breakfast he fed them every morning. I was tempted to try a similar menu but, combined with 'My Sharona', I felt it could be the first step on the road to an eccentricity I wasn't yet ready to embrace. The Bear had enjoyed broccoli in the past, but any time I'd tried to give it to Janet he'd looked at me with abject horror. However, slowly but surely, he was beginning to regain his appetite.

It's hard to pinpoint exactly when Janet started to get slightly better. One answer would be 'around the same time I did'. There was no sudden epiphany or recovery for either of us, but by late summer 2009, you would have noticed a slight change in our demeanour: a lifting of our spirits. The upping of the dosage of Janet's pills had – when I could actually get them inside him – worked. In the vet's words, he was 'never going to become Arnold Schwarzenegger' but he had regained a considerable amount of weight. I'm sure a part of him would hold a grudge against me forever for what

I'd done to him, but I noticed him softening to my touch, once again rubbing a cold nose against my dangling hand to wake me up in the morning, and asking me for one of his favourite chest massages. I also noticed that his wrestles with Shipley had resumed, and he seemed to be holding his own. Perhaps he'd lost his position as Top Cat, but if Shipley got too full of himself, Ralph would soon put him in his place with a swift headlock, like the crybaby psychopath he was.

Another side effect of Janet's resurgence was the curbing of his litter habit. The drying up of the supply of empty Rizla and Chippy Chips packets in the garden was gradual, and seemed to occur in direct correlation to the improvement in his health. This seemed to confirm my suspicions that the main root of Janet's wombling had not been a wish to be part of the Keep Britain Tidy campaign, or some bizarre autistic attachment to inanimate objects, but a mysterious conviction that they contained a cure. But what? I felt that, if The Bear could speak, he would have been able to tell me. He'd so often been around during the hard times with Janet – his most violent vomiting sessions, those moments when he gargled and clawed at me as I tried to push the pill into the back of his mouth, and the time when I found him sprawled out in the kitchen, whining mournfully next to an algae-coated monstrosity that, many waterlogged years ago, had probably had another life as a small swing-bin liner. At these times, The Bear would usually be found observing us from some high perch, wryly. As Janet faded, he'd become almost preposterously plush, as if he was sucking the life force from his fluffier companion. One day, a newspaper photographer arrived at the house, looked at The Bear, and said, 'I assume this is one of the younger ones?' I asked him to guess his age. 'Three?' he said.

There would still be much pain in the aftermath of my split with Dee. And with it loomed the spectre of Jake from Texas: the single man in late middle age, with no cat boundaries. I can't say it was an appealing future. On the other hand, I had always quite fancied living in a shack, so it wouldn't be without its upside. Soon, Dee would be moving into a flat with a garden, and we would have to go through the agony of dividing our cats. The exact vagaries of who ended up living with whom had not been decided yet, but it looked very much like The Bear and Janet – the cats I'd inherited from her – would be living with me. 'Those two have always liked you better than me anyway,' she reasoned.

But did The Bear and Janet like *each other*? I'm not sure 'like' was quite the right word. Fate would often look like splitting up their Odd Couple relationship, then throw them back together, usually to The Bear's chagrin and Janet's brief, dumb excitement. They were slightly jaded by one another, perhaps not as *interested* in one another as other cats in their vicinity, but it was surprising how often they ended up on the same bed or sofa, just a matter of inches from touching tails. They were very different characters, but they were different from my other cats too: a little less demanding, a little less spoilt. And then there was their strange pacifism: I still had no evidence that either of them had ever slaughtered another living thing.

Was that what Janet had been doing, during the early days of his thyroid troubles, when he'd been so hungry? Looking for nourishment in litter? I liked to think so: that, despite being ravenous, it was his way of doing all he could and not let his resolve crumble and go and pick off a sickly field mouse or tired jackdaw. And I also liked to think that this was why, despite the odds, he had earned The Bear's respect. It was a rather colourful, imaginative theory, admittedly, but perhaps no more so than the other ones I clung to, to sustain my belief that my cats were higher beings, cogitators and plotters: superior animals worthy of a special respect, and the deferment of our own, slightly inferior lives.

Animals I Have Not Really Been That Bothered About Stealing. Number One: 'Street' Moorhen

NAME:
Mo'hen

OCCUPATION:
Scampering, generally being coot-esque

HOME:
South Norfolk, UK

BRIEF CV:
Moorhen was like, 'You wanna piece of me?' And I was like, 'No, you're a moorhen.' And moorhen was like, 'I'm just gonna cross this road, just you watch me.' And I was like, 'Okay, I'll slow down to 15mph – in many ways North

Lopham should be a 20 zone anyway.' And moorhen was like, 'That's what I'm talking about – how do you like me now?' And then we both passed safely on our way, without further incident.

Oh, Whistle and There's a Vague Chance I Might Come to You m'lad: The Diary of an Amateur Dog Walker

14 January 2009

Today Dee and I went for a walk with Hannah, Dee's friend from work who has just moved in up the road, and Hannah's cocker spaniel, Henry. 'Hannah might even let you walk him, if you're lucky,' Dee told me, as we waited outside Hannah's front door. It's been a few years since my regular walks with Nouster, the Border collie owned by our former neighbours Richard and Kath, so I was thrilled at the prospect of having a new dog in my life.

'Really?' I asked. 'Are you sure?'

'Are you . . . panting?' said Dee.

'No,' I protested. 'I'm just a bit wheezy, what with the cold.'

The four of us set off down the hill, leading out of East Mendleham past the old fairground site, Henry pulling Hannah along at quite a pace. 'He's not fully trained yet,' she said breathlessly. Henry is a cocker spaniel, but he is so big he is usually mistaken for the next breed up: a springer. He is black with white splotches and has mischievous, red eyes that seem to glow even redder as he makes a dastardly beeline for ducks and pedestrians carrying freshly wrapped chips.

'You'll be okay,' Hannah said. 'He likes men.' One of the men Henry showed a liking for on this occasion was a hobo, living in the woods beside the heath, where the river cuts in, about a mile from East Mendleham. 'Henry! Come back here! No! Leave that man alone!' Hannah shouted. She and Dee seemed nervous, but I was impressed as the hobo came out from beneath his tarpaulin to see what all the fuss was about. His weather-beaten hawkish face looked startled, with no evidence of the usual jumpy smile of the person who gets accosted by a dog in the British countryside.

East Mendleham is not without its colourful transients. The man with the overalls and the David Crosby hair who sits beside the town lake all day and reads nineteenth-century French literature has long intrigued me, and I suppose, if you like that kind of thing and don't have to make a living from writing in the nearby vicinity, the old man with the badge-covered blazer who shouted, 'Fucking come on then! Let's be having you!' at the town ducks every morning has his pluses. But, whatever terrible tragedy had put you there, however down on your luck you were, choosing to bed down in the middle of the countryside was something else: the act of an iconoclast.

I didn't want to get too close and disturb the hobo's business – and he definitely looked like he had some – but I found myself peering over, curious about the paraphernalia of his life. What were those papers next to his campfire? Old pamphlets of some kind, containing the wisdom of previous hobos from many years before? Or just his special Hobo's Diary? Actually, getting a bit closer, they looked more like the last couple of issues of GQ magazine. But what did he cook? What did he spend his days thinking about? Did his voice taste odd in his mouth on the rare occasions he communicated with another human being? Hannah and Dee looked relieved as Henry trotted back over to us, but I was thinking forward to my and Henry's mutual future, uncovering the eccentrics of the East Anglian countryside.

I took Henry's lead as we turned for home. He was smaller than Nouster had been, but I was struck by his strength, particularly when he found the rotting ribcage of some sizable road kill on the verge of the road, and decided he would like nothing better than to wriggle on top of it on his back. This kind of animal communion with the deceased was new to me. My cats have killed plenty of creatures, of course, but after a couple of scissor kicks and a bit of juggling they usually lose interest in their rodent victims. You might find them neatly severing a shrew's spleen and placing it on the carpet outside my bedroom, as a child might leave the crusts from his bread for a parent to clean away, but you wouldn't have caught them using it as a pillow later.

'Oh, yes, that's happened before,' said Hannah. 'He sat on a dead pheasant the other day.'

Before heading home, we stopped at the local pub, and I congratulated Henry on being a good boy – I wasn't actually sure that he *had* been a good boy, not being aware of the previous standards set, but it felt like the polite thing to do – and ordered us each a pint of Guinness and a packet of cheese and onion crisps. I was about to dip my hand into the latter, but remembered just in time to go to the bathroom, lest I fatally mix rotting ribcage with cheese powder, vegetable oil and salt. As we drank, Hannah and Dee taught me some spaniel terms, from the spaniel-heavy office of the horse charity where the two of them work. A tail, apparently, was known by insiders as 'wagstick'. The curly scribble of hair on Henry's dome was officially termed his 'dogwig'.

'It's like I told Tom after I'd first met Henry,' Dee said to Hannah. '"You'll love this spaniel. He's almost exactly like you, only he's a spaniel."'

It wasn't the first time I'd been compared to a dog, and in this specific instance, I could see the physical evidence on hand. Since my mid-teens, I've had dark, thickish curly hair. Over recent years this has receded slightly at the temples, leaving something of a fluffy peninsula at the front; I can assure you that it's 100 per cent natural, but I suppose, in spaniel vernacular, you could call it my own sort of dogwig. I was fine with that. Still, considering that the observation had come from the person I spent most of my time with, and who had also just used the term 'simpleton' and 'galumphing' in describing Henry, I could not help dwelling on it slightly, as we walked home.

23 January 2009

I hear from Hannah that, on his walks, as he passes The Upside Down House, Henry has been pulling her towards the front door. I could hardly believe this could be the case, as he'd only been to visit us once, but as I brought him down to my car, from Hannah's house, before setting off on our first walk together alone, he seemed to know where he was going. I decided not to let him in, for fear of alienating the cats, who already seem to sense something is not quite right.

Henry, I'm told, can get a little bit antsy in the car when traffic is slow, tending to howl whenever Hannah's speedometer slips below 30mph: a kind of dog version of the movie *Speed*, but with a spaniel instead of a bomb and a Nissan Micra in place of a bus. If so, he was on good behaviour, only beginning to whimper impatiently as we arrived at our destination, Dunwich, on the Suffolk coast.

One of my New Year's resolutions four weeks ago was to try to complete fifty-two East Anglian walks of four miles or above, in an attempt to get to know my local area better, an endeavour for which I have purchased a deerstalker hat, and grown a winter beard. They say the most important part of the body to keep warm is the head and this hat is so absurdly furry, I sense that it doesn't actually matter what I'm wearing, I'll still be warm in it. This is, however, a theory I'm somewhat reluctant to test out in full.

One thing I've noticed about being a lone bearded man, walking through remote countryside wearing novelty headgear, is that you are not always automatically viewed as a wholesome figure. You can tell from the shift of your fellow walkers' gaze as you pass them. Add a dog to the equation, however, and everything changes. As I walked Henry along the beach at Dunwich, everyone I saw stopped to exchange hearty hellos with us. 'Is he a springer?' a fellow spaniel-walker, a ruddy-cheeked, blonde lady in wellies and a Barbour jacket, asked.

'No, just a big cocker,' I replied, with a certain smug sense of assurance.

That I can now utter phrases like 'big cocker' without feeling the need to giggle is perhaps a measure of how far I've already come in my short time as a dog walker. Nevertheless, I remained nervous about further questioning from the Barbour-jacketed lady. What if she asked me about what products I used to clean him, or where I got his lead? I am unconvinced that my bluffing would be able to withstand such interrogation. I am also aware that when I call Henry, and put him back on his lead, I am not just doing so to prevent problematic encounters between him and other dogs; I am also doing so to prevent scenarios where, by being forced to make conversation with doggy types, my phoniness will be revealed.

I'm usually pretty good at getting Henry re-leashed, and he does always tend to scuttle back to me the second or third time I call him, but upon spotting a Labrador on the woodland track back from the Dunwich marshes, I acted a little slowly. There was a small barking exchange, and the Lab's owner and I exchanged a nervous glance, before the Lab wibbled off, visibly upset, and Henry scuttled back to me. I noticed three main thoughts going round my head as I wandered back to the car:

1. 'I probably would have handled that better if I hadn't owned cats instead of dogs my whole life.'
2. 'I must watch out for Henry's bullying streak.'
3. 'My dog kicked another, bigger dog's butt. Awesome!'

12 February 2009
Hannah and I seem to have come to a happy arrangement very easily, regarding Henry's walks. When Hannah is away on a business trip, I will do my best to walk Henry, and can

pretty much walk him any other time I please, so long as I give her at least a day's notice. Hannah seems grateful for this, which is odd, since it's she who's doing me the larger favour. The bonuses are twofold: I get a quick-fix confidence boost for when my cats are treating me even more like a doormat than usual, and dog ownership without the hassle – or so it would seem. Yes, I have to pick up Henry's excrement, and reward him with biscuits and chews, but I do not have to clean Henry, buy food for him, take care of his vet bills, or listen to his whining at night. As someone who's toyed with the idea of getting a dog recently, I also am getting a perfect trial run for dog ownership.

This is not to say that I am able to keep my time with Henry completely compartmentalised from the rest of my life. During today's walk near Burnham Overy Staithe, on the North Norfolk coast, Henry jumped into the river several times, and smelled distinctly ripe in the car afterwards. Later, having dropped Henry home, I collected my friends Steve and Sue from the train station. Our subsequent conversation is the second time I have apologised for the fact that my car 'smells of spaniel'.

28 February 2009

Henry pissed on his paws again this afternoon. I'm told by Dee that this is because he has a slightly arthritic hip, and cannot cock his leg properly. To be frank, I'm still coming to terms with spending time with an animal who is not entirely self-sufficient, in terms of his own bowel functions, and further alarm comes from his habit of taking a dump in the exact middle of country lanes, usually a matter of seconds before a four-by-four comes haring around the nearest bend. Today, a few miles south of Norwich, near the village of

Loddon, I was almost mown down by a Range Rover as I dived for Henry's excrement, baggy in hand, and rolled skillfully over into a roadside ditch. Henry, however, appeared unmoved by the incident, and raced off to intimidate some ducks. There's still a part of me that, as I carry his poo in a plastic bag, in my coat pocket, is asking myself, 'You mean people actually *choose* to do this? *Every day?*' Sometimes, as we walk, I'll forget about the bag, and think about how the brisk Broadland breeze feels against my skin, or admire a scarecrow in a nearby field, but my sense of its presence never fully goes away and, somehow, as I walk further, that presence seems to expand, until I feel I am walking with not just one living creature, but two.

18 March 2009
Number of animals encountered on walk today by Henry and me: seventeen. Number of animals wound up by Henry: fourteen.

24 March 2009
When Henry and I walk locally, there are now various neighbourhood dogs we have come to recognise. For these, we like to make-up appropriate nicknames. Well, I say, 'we'; I obviously mean 'I', but I feel that, if Henry could make up nicknames for his canine rivals, he would take great pleasure in doing so. I suppose he's quite a lippy, boisterous dog, and I can see that his goading and cheek can get easily on the nerves of a snotty Dalmatian or a well-heeled wolfhound, but at least he's not aloof or imperious in any way, and is as happy to say hello to a Jack Russell as he is to a greyhound. This is more than I can say for the Janetdog, so named by me because of its striking resemblance to my cat Janet. The

Janetdog strutted past us, snout in the air, fluffy tail high, this afternoon and you could just tell we were no more than a couple of dirty specks on its radar. This seems pretty rich, coming from a creature that looks like one of the most brainless felines in East Anglia.

7 April 2009

I think I am becoming more commanding in my instructions to Henry. I can almost feel my voice getting inadvertently deeper when I shout him. Dee, meanwhile, has taken to calling him my 'alter doggo'. I'm choosing to take this as largely a reference to my walking hat, and its spaniel-style ears. He's still a little slow in coming to me, but he *does* always come, eventually. There are moments, like the one a couple of hours ago, on the heath a mile from home, where I was almost passing myself off as a proper dog owner. The illusion was only shattered when Henry began having a 'conversation' with two Border collies and a red setter. Was it the item of mod clothing my dad calls 'YOUR NANCY BOY COAT' that blew it for me? Or my shout of 'Hey! Leave those ever-so-slightly bigger dogs alone!'? Weighty arguments, no doubt, exist for both.

2 May 2009

Henry has had an accident. While staying at Hannah's parents' house last week, he broke into their kitchen bin, despite the fact that, as a precaution for precisely such an eventuality, said rubbish receptacle had been weighted down with two bricks. During this adventure, Henry managed to eat 2.5kg of old food, tissues, cellophane wrappers, and some leftover Chinese ribs. This has resulted in what

Hannah has described as 'a blockage', leading to an operation, and stitches. Henry is currently being carried around
the office in one of the blue woven plastic bags customers
pick up near the entrance of IKEA, though Hannah assures
me that this does not stop him from attempting to jump up
and 'go for the ties' of executive male members of staff.

19 May 2009
Am I now officially hound-friendly? It would seem so. This
afternoon I walked, Henryless, between the Norfolk villages
of Castle Acre and West Acre. After a mile or two, I passed
by a welcoming-looking pub, with 'Don't Spook the Horse:
7.30' written on a sign outside. I couldn't work out if this
served as an advertisement for some live music, or just as a
general instruction for the welfare of passers-by. No horse
emerged, but a small brown mongrel – the kind of dog a
person finds himself wanting to call 'Rascal' – did, then followed me down a lane leading to a ford. I attempted to shoo
him back, but he seemed quite determined, and continued
to walk a few paces ahead of me. There was a presumption
about this on his part, as if this had all been prearranged by
a third party: his dark lord and master, perhaps, who lived in
a cave at the end of the footpath he now led me along.

This point in my seven-mile route involved a number of
stiles, twists, turns and cross-field paths, but Rascal, keeping
pace ahead of me, seemed familiar with it, and needed no
instruction. I passed another couple of ramblers, and, if they
could sense that he was not my dog, they didn't show it. But
I worried. What if we passed Jim and Mary from the village,
for example, and they wanted to know what the strange
bloke with the beard was doing with Brian the Landlord's
dog?

What if Jim was a nosy type, known for his interfering ways and bad poetry in the parish newsletter? I could imagine the accusations of theft, the subsequent trial, with Hannah standing on the witness stand, a betrayed look across her face, confessing, 'Well, I do admit I thought it was a *bit* strange when he told me he was into borrowing dogs, but I thought he seemed trustworthy enough. Now, though, I realise I was naive.'

Rascal and I must have walked a full mile before he turned around and scuttled home, in a manner no more explicable than the one in which he'd joined me. After that, I only saw two more dogs on the walk, and neither of them followed me, though one, a Briard, did leap up and put its muddy paws on my chest. This seemed a more familiar canine perception of me: not as companion, but as the kind of sap who would smile, chuckle nervously and not complain if he got a big load of crud all over his Tom Petty and the Heartbreakers t-shirt.

25 June 2009

Henry seemed fully recovered when I collected him today. With the addition of a sleek haircut – the dogwig is gone, and I can't pretend I don't miss it – he actually looks healthier than ever. When I arrived at Hannah's, he commenced his usual routine, with no noticeable difficulty; this involves him stealing his lead from my hand, then running in maniacal circles for three or four minutes before he allows me to attach it. I then stroke and pat him, and he seems to enjoy it, but here I miss the feedback I receive from my cats. I have no idea whether I'm rubbing him up the wrong way or the right way and I suspect he doesn't care.

'Are all dogs like this?' I wonder. I know you don't get

purring dogs, but surely some canines are a little more dis-
cerning, and offer a more comprehensive appraisal of your
affections. Having said that, I'm yet to meet one. I suppose
this says a lot about why I'm a cat owner. I love dogs, but I'm
not sure if I truly respect them. They're too easily pleased,
and their judgement offers no true preparation for the trials
of real life.

Some of this is undoubtedly down to intelligence. Dogs
chase cats in the folklore of cartoons, but the reality is rarely
as simple. In almost every household I know containing
dogs and cats, the cats have the upper hand. In the vicinity
of my last house, there were few sights more satisfying than
watching my neighbour Jenny's little dog Tansy trying it on
with Jenny's hulking black moggy Spooky, then getting a
sound paw-slapping for her trouble. Even if a dog such as
Henry came to live with my cats and retained the physical
upper hand, the labyrinthine complexity of their mind
games would soon get the better of him.

Nonetheless, I am not sure you could call Henry completely stupid. Evidence of a primal and mysterious intellect
of some form can certainly be found in the timing of his
whimpering on our car journeys. I still haven't experienced
the obsession with speed that Hannah warned me about
early on, but I have noticed that a couple of minutes before
I park the car at our destination, be begins to squeak and pip
excitedly. Take today, for example: I've checked with
Hannah, and I know Henry has never before visited the
enchanting Arts and Crafts village of Thorpeness, on the
Suffolk coast, yet from a few minutes before I pulled into
Leiston Leisure Centre car park, where our walking route
started, his familiar chorus began.

This is not merely a matter of him responding to the

slowing of the car. I slow the car down plenty of times on our journeys – sometimes I even stop for petrol – and Henry barely stirs. But, in Henry's mind, who is to say I'm not going to stop and walk him round a petrol station? This seems evidence of a different extreme stupidity/crafty intelligence dichotomy to the one found in cats, but it does seem to share something in common: the overwhelming sense that an animal is reading my mind.

16 July 2009
Perks of dog borrowing, #173: So far this week I have used the phrase 'I'm sorry, you'll have to forgive me: my car smells of spaniel' three times. My car does not actually smell of spaniel. It is just very dirty.

3 August 2009
My walking regime for this year means that I've also been doing something I haven't done with any regularity for two decades: rambling through the countryside with my parents. This is rather unnerving for them, as it occurs without me asking, 'How long is it to go *now*?' or lagging behind them and practising my golf swing, and rather alarming for me, as there's a thirteen-year-old part of me that still feels it's my duty to not enjoy walking with my parents and to ask, 'How long is it to go *now*?' and lag behind them practising my golf swing.

I've been a bit slow in taking Henry on a walk with my mum and dad. Not that I could remotely imagine Henry scaring any human being, but my dad was bitten by an Alsatian when he was young, and has a slightly fractious relationship with dogs as a result. This is a shame, because in many ways, a pet dog of his own would be a perfect

apprentice for my dad: a creature who could look up ador-
ingly and non-judgmentally at him as he makes a succession
of wordplay-based jokes and campaigns evangelically to get
everyone around him to listen to the Radio 4 *News Quiz*.
My canine world is one where you say, 'Hello!' to dogs in a
posh voice, they say hello back to you, then move along
their way, or at the very worst, smear their paws on your new
Aerosmith t-shirt. My dad's, by contrast, is one where
snarling East Midlands men in baseball caps say, 'Don't
worry, mate, 'e not hurt you' a split second before their
Rottweiler gnaws chunks out of your cheek.

I often suggest to my mum that she and my dad get a dog,
and not just because, having now got a taste for dog borrowing, I am actually fantasising about building myself a
network of canines available for my use at a succession of
evenly spread points across the British Isles. I tell them it
would suit their lifestyle well, and would be a brilliant addition to their walks.

'Ooh no, I don't think it would work,' my mum says.
'Life's already too complicated as it is. And I don't know if
your dad would really like it.'

It would be an understatement on a par with many of his
own overstatements to say that my dad is prone to exagger-
ation, but I can see there's truth in what he says: dogs and he
do appear to have some insurmountable issues. It's as if they
both come into each encounter knowing the mutual history
of their breeds. My dad and dogs don't just nod and go along
with their business. When they cross paths, Things Happen.
Just a month ago when he was walking in Cambridgeshire,
my dad found a stray golden retriever wandering through a
meadow. Not spotting any owner around, he removed his
belt from his baggy cord trousers, tied it around the retriever's

neck, and began to lead it back towards a nearby village, in an attempt to find its owner. A mile further on, he was surprised to find a woman in wellies in her mid-forties charging up to him, accusing him of stealing her beloved pet.

When my dad walks, he invariably carries with him a 'dog dazer', in case of emergencies: a handheld device that emits ultrasonic sound waves that stun aggressive dogs into submission. I made him promise to leave this at home for our walk with Henry at Blakeney Point today.

'HE'S NOT GOING TO ATTACK ME IS HE?' he said as Henry jumped out of the boot of my car enthusiastically in the quayside car park.

'No, no. You'll be fine,' I said, and pretty soon the two of them were striding out over the salt marshes together, forty paces ahead of my mum and me. Perhaps in consideration of the immense unspoilt natural beauty of this stretch of the North Norfolk coastline, Henry opted to wait to empty his bowels until we had looped back to the main road, leaving me crouched down on the white line, hurriedly bagging up the contents as a BMW 7 Series came snaking into view at 60mph.

'WHAT ARE YOU GOING TO DO WITH THAT?' asked my dad, when I had dragged myself to the grass verge.

'I'm going to put it inside my bag until I find one of those special dog bins for it,' I replied.

'OOH FOOKTIVANO. YOU'RE BLOODY JOKING. THAT'S HORRIBLE.'

It was a hot day, and, though the excrement was double polythened, then placed in the relative cool of my shoulder bag, I felt an acute sense of it changing texture as we walked on. It really did seem an awful long time between dog bins. I chose to remain a model citizen for the time being, and keep the offending item in my bag, but I could definitely see the appeal of hurling it full toss into a nearby field, and the liberation that would follow: me striding off into the sun, a shit-free knapsack on my shoulder, all my worries behind me.

After about five miles, we came to a stile. The fencing was a little low, and Henry looked up at me, expectantly, and I lifted him over.

'DO YOU ALWAYS HAVE TO DO THAT?' said my dad.

'I do if he can't go underneath,' I said. 'He's a bit arthritic.'

'I SUPPOSE YOU COULD SAY YOU WERE DOING IT DOGGY STILE.'

By now I've learned that Henry is drawn to loud people and, perhaps for this reason, he tended to gravitate towards my dad. Earlier, as we'd stopped beside the marsh for a picnic, my dad had even shared some pork pie with him. You'd have to know my dad, who is notoriously cautious about sharing meat, even with some of his best friends and closest relatives, to realise what kind of a breakthrough this was. Once again I talked about how well a dog of their own might suit my parents' lifestyle, and what a great addition it would be to their walks. However, as fond as they seemed of Henry, they seemed unconvinced, and my dad, in particular, didn't seem to be listening.

'KEEP IN!' he shouted as each car passed us on the narrow country lane.

It was an extremely useful instruction, under the circumstances. After all, what with my mum and I not being scheduled to start our first term as primary school pupils for another two months, and not yet having any road sense, either one of us could have wandered blithely out in front of a car at any time without his crucial guardianship.

'Mick,' said my mum. 'You don't have to shout that every time a car comes.'

'WHAT? I CAN'T BELIEVE IT. THE TWO OF YOU ARE ALWAYS PICKING ON ME,' said my dad.

A mile or so later, as we turned onto a heath-land path, I gently suggested that an earlier right turn might have led to an even more scenic route.

'WHAT ARE YOU TALKING ABOUT?' said my dad. 'I WAS GOING ON COUNTRY WALKS BEFORE YOU WERE BORN.'

He was beginning to sulk now. In retrospect, I probably went too far in following up by asking him if he was 'the man who invented walking'. I felt guilty, as I always do when I've been sarcastic towards him. On the upside, Henry was looking up at him with undiluted admiration. I couldn't help thinking back to the photos I'd seen of my dad as a teenager, in so many of which he seemed to be pulling a kind of proto-punk, mocking face at the camera, and also of something Hannah had said about Henry: 'I swear if this dog had fingers on the end of his paws, he'd spend most of his life sticking two of them up.' Watching them picking up the pace and walking back towards the salt marshes ahead of us and thinking about the dog dazer and the Alsatian bite, you might have initially thought it was an unlikely meeting of the minds, but when you considered it more deeply, there was something very right about it.

3 August 2009
Email from my mum: 'Lovely to see you. Was really great meeting Henry. We both loved him. We're actually thinking

of getting a dog now. Your dad thinks it would really suit our lifestyle, in a way, and make our walks even more interesting.'

Sent reply: 'Really? I suppose I had never thought of it that way. I probably should have suggested it.'

7 August 2009

Have not seen Henry for a few days and am, just for the first time, missing him slightly. Received update from Hannah, to tide me over: a photograph of him happily licking an ice cream, and the news that, yesterday, he attempted to swing from her CEO's tie.

10 August 2009

Further Henry update from Hannah, who has now noticed that all the executives at work have started tucking their ties into their trousers, and fears it may not be just a trend.

14 August 2009

Update from mum: my dad has decided not to get a dog after all, having been slightly harassed by a Dobermann on today's walk, but has, instead, bought a really fat new fish for his pond.

17 August 2009

Henry attempted to eat a man's chips today on the seafront at Aldeburgh. 'Get down, Henry!' I shouted, surprising myself with my authority.

'Yes, Henry, I'm afraid I can't give you any of these,' said the man, politely. I apologised, he complimented Henry on his red eyes, and pointed out his own dog, a Dachshund, who was up ahead, gambolling in the surf with his wife.

Each time I walk Henry I am more aware of the way he connects me to my fellow humans. When you walk alone in the countryside, you are a bit of loose debris floating through the abyss, but when you walk with a dog, that debris becomes a sticky bud with the potential to briefly or not so briefly fasten itself to someone else. While walking Henry, I realise that those romantic comedies where souls collide in the local park over a fracas between the male party's Coonhound and the female party's Beagle are not just the stuff of Hollywood fantasy. They can really happen! It only remains a shame, perhaps, that I am not in the market for a 17-stone, married, bald man with an oversized 1980s ski jacket and a probable connection with the Countryside Alliance.

29 August 2009
Possible entry for *Dog Dictionary*: 'Unitard: a uniquely lovable kind of retard.'

5 September 2009
I remain fascinated as to why every time Henry jumps in a broad or river or dyke or marsh, no matter how deep or dirty, he smells precisely the same. Surely Norfolk and Suffolk's waterways have a mind-bogglingly eclectic variety of pollution, dead insects, animal death juice, excrement and rainwater in them? Hence, they would each have their own original smells. So how come, having reacted with Henry, they always result in the same damp doggy pong: an odour that, though not evil, has a boisterousness about it that tends to pen a person in. My feeling is that this is a dis-tinction to be proud of, in dog terms. I suppose you could look at Henry as a kind of olfactory version of the unique

and mesmerising actor Christopher Walken: you can put him with any kind of accompaniment, however watered down, but you're still going to know he's Henry.

17 September 2009

After what happened to Henry when he raided Hannah's parents' bin earlier in the year, I'm very vigilant about watching his eating habits, which, from what I can work out, seem to extend to anything that isn't another dog or a human, but sometimes I'm just not quick enough. My cats will vigilantly check any foodstuff offered to them for poison, arsenic and poor craftsmanship before proceeding, but Henry's packed itinerary does not allow for that. During our latest walk, he not only licked the trunk of a tree, but managed to consume something unidentifiable in a chip wrapper that almost certainly wasn't chips, and a half-eaten Cornish pasty bought from the Westward Ho! branch of the Co-op on a golf holiday of mine seven weeks previously, which had somehow secreted itself beneath the divider in the boot of my car. This, however, might be less of a damning comment about Henry's diet than it is about how my standards of automobile maintenance have slipped since becoming a part-time spaniel walker.

28 September 2009

Today my friend Jess and I went for a walk with Henry, and Jess's farm collie, Spartacus, at Knettishall Heath, on the edge of Thetford Forest. The two dogs got on pretty well, and it was clear that Spartacus wasn't going to let any of Henry's lip get to him. As my first dual dog walk, it was instructive in showing me just how far I've travelled as a dog borrower, but just what little distance I've really come. I made a perfunctory effort at shouting Henry back for the first mile, but by the time we'd walked for half an hour, I'd happily ceded the disciplining of both dogs to Jess. Jess is a vet, hence kills things almost every day, so she's made of tougher stuff than me, but I sense the situation would have been the same with 99 per cent of fellow dog owners. Dogs see me as a kindred idiot spirit, I sense, but I'm also sure they can see through my half-hearted attempts to be their master. This goes right back to the time I was ten, and used to hang out in the garden of my neighbour Dorothy Cope, and wrestle with her black Labrador, Bella, and whippet-cross, Millie: a playful meeting of equals, rather than an early exercise in command and control. I've spent a considerable amount of time with Henry now, but I'm not sure I'm any closer to actually wanting a dog of my own; I just know I really like having a dog of my own to borrow.

3 October 2009
Today could well be the last warm day of the year, so, perhaps rather ambitiously, I took Henry to the village of Blythburgh, for a special, nine-mile Black Shuck walk. Shuck is a legend of the Suffolk coast: a ghostly black dog, the size of a small horse, who roamed the nearby countryside from pre-Viking times, and, in 1577, broke into Blythburgh Church, terrorising the congregation and killing two of its number. As I looked at what are allegedly the scratch marks he left on the north door, I wondered if my own borrowed black dog would be capable of anything similar. It seemed unlikely, though I could definitely picture him being quite intimidating in his mission to steal the parishioners' post-service cakes and muffins.

Our walk took us on a loop inland, then back towards the

coast, following the River Blyth. Midway, we stopped at a
deserted pub whose owners had kindly put a bowl of water
outside the front door to appease thirsty passing black dogs.
I've been walking Henry for nine months now, and I still
haven't been brave enough to tie him up outside a shop or
a pub yet. This is because, as a rule, I view knots with suspi-
cion, and tend to shy away from them if given the
opportunity. With this in mind, I attempted to carry a pint
of Adnams bitter and some cheese and chive flavoured
crisps in one hand, while wielding Henry's lead from the
other. In retrospect, it was probably for the best that half of
my drink ended up on the floor, as I was quite tired by this
point, and needed all my faculties for the remainder of the
walk.

One of the best things about the route I'd chosen is that
the spire of Blythburgh church, where the walk had begun
and ended, serves as a marker. As Henry and I walked
towards it, even he looked a little fatigued, which I'd previously thought impossible. I'd worn the wrong kind of socks
with my normally comfortable walking boots, and I could
feel a blister on my heel swelling with, and possibly leaking,
blood. The spire came closer and closer into view, but something seemed wrong about the directions: there'd been no
left turn through the reeds where I'd imagined it and, with
the River Blyth continuing on our left with no break, there
appeared to be no alternative footpath.

I've learned by now that my walking books are not always
factually correct in their distances. Also, the AA series of
British walkers' manuals, in particular, can get a little emo-
tive in their language sometimes. 'Strike out across a field'
always seems a rather dramatic description of the act of
walking diagonally, at a rather sedate pace, across some mud

scattered with rotten cabbages. Meanwhile, 'jig left, then right, passing curious sows in their pens' is downright hysterical, unless you're one of that special breed of ramblers who spontaneously explodes into dance every time you see an inquisitive pig. But I tend to let that kind of thing go. This, however, was ridiculous: wherever we looked, Henry and I could not find a footpath. For almost an hour we wandered aimlessly through reeds and river meadows, looking for a way across the river. As we did so, the grey spire of Black Shuck's church served as a kind of doomful upright rainbow: we walked towards it, but we never got any closer.

Never having owned dogs, but having a fair appreciation of fictional canines, I was hoping that Henry might take charge of the situation, perhaps angling his head, saying 'Rowwwf?' then 'Rowwwf rowwf!' and leading me to safety, but he didn't seem too concerned, and preoccupied himself with jumping repeatedly in the river and making a nearby heron soil itself. It would be dark in under two hours, a dusk chill was already in the air, and the pain in my foot had become so excruciating, I had taken my shoes off to reveal a grey sock soaked completely red. But what if I became stranded out here in the dark? I was suddenly acutely aware of my status as a single person. Who would I send my SOS message to? In desperation, I posted a message on the social networking site Twitter: 'Lost in Suffolk countryside. If this is the last you hear from me, please let it be known that "Fairground" by Simply Red was my least favourite song of all time.'

I was, though, genuinely worried; I was not just responsible for me, but for a dog who – if there wasn't a chip shop in the vicinity – seemed to have little concept of fending for himself.

Finally, buried amid some bullrushes, I found a sign, explaining that, due to the river walls breaking down, the footpaths in the area had been flooded and lost. The only available route back to the car involved turning back the way we'd come and taking a four-mile detour. Upon reaching the last couple of stiles, Henry looked weary, for the first time since I'd known him, and I obligingly carried him over them. By the time we reached the car, we'd walked fourteen miles in total, and the sky above Black Shuck's church was dark and foreboding, although perhaps not as dark and foreboding as my blister, which from a cursory glance, now measured exactly one-and-a-half times the size of my foot. By chance, as I pulled out of the car park, the shuffle function on my iPod selected the song 'Black Shuck' by the rock band The Darkness, who originally hail from down the road from here. 'Black Shuck!' howled the singer, in his rock falsetto. The next line was a rhyming reference to the thing that the dog in question didn't give: a popular Anglo-Saxon curse word, with Germanic roots, still in common use today. Behind me, in the back seat, my own temporary black dog slept through it all – a much more positive influence than the black dogs of legend, but evidently in his own way equally capable of not giving the same thing.

Some Random Selections from the Cat Dictionary

Air Scratch
To flail wildly and absurdly at the air with one's back leg as one's owner attempts to 'help' scratch an itch that, in all honesty, thanks all the same and everything, you had perfectly well covered. Some say the air scratch is not as involuntary as it seems, and is actually an obscene gesture whose roots stretch back as far as ancient Egypt: a kind of feline version of a two-fingered salute, but much, much ruder. Others just decry it as another forlorn symbol of man's increasing interference in cat culture, a debasement of nature that will ultimately send us on a road to a dark place where a word like 'natural' no longer even has any meaning.

Catgut
The quality of feline true grit in the face of adversity. For example: managing to stoically wait out the twenty minutes between the biscuit dispenser becoming empty and your

human serf abandoning his overdue, half-finished piece of journalism to hotfoot it down to the pet store for replacement supplies.

DSDASIGHGDSHSDDC

Feline scholars are split upon estimating when the ancient language of dsdasighgdshsddc first emerged. Some put the date around about 1983, during the rise of the BBC Micro and the ZX Spectrum home computers. Others claim that techno geek cats in San Francisco's South Park district were communicating in it as far back as 1974. Whatever the case, it is generally agreed that dsdasighgdshsddc has been in regular use since the early 90s. While often written off by humans as a random, unintentional series of letters generated by the patter of mischievous paws across a keyboard, what many people don't know is that dsdasighgdshsddc actually forms an entire exclamatory, often insult-heavy, feline language: a kind of profane moggy binary, if you like, being sent to other cats across the globe via a complex email system invisible to the human eye. Popular examples of dsdasighgdshsddc 'dissing' include auoagfoylhgo ('Eat my tail scum!') and oiaiuhagiuggghafug ('Your mum was a Griffon Bruxellois!'). Of course, with the rise of the Internet, dsdasighgdshsddc has evolved, mutated and, some would claim, been irrevocably dumbed down. For example, jhjdhjdhddddddvvvd ('Oh my god! How much do I want my owner to get off this computer and let me pad his stomach!') is now lazily abbreviated by many Generation Y cats to a simpler, less poetic jhdvvvvd.

Grudgin

A half-hearted version of the Nuggin, the act of pushing one's wet nose into one's human's hand or knuckle (see

Under the Paw, Simon & Schuster, 2008), The Grudgin more often than not marks a bargain between cat and owner: 'I am feeling too bored/self-important/generally unarsed to push the side of my nose into your hand, but will do so, half-heartedly, knowing that this is the price one must pay for leftover, past-its-sell-by-date, wafer-thin turkey.'

Litebeer
The kind of middling, tepid water still bafflingly placed by humans for cats in a combination of receptacles all over the globe, in spite of empirical evidence suggesting that the favourite tipple of most felines is either a) water straight from the tap, or b) stagnant pond soup, seasoned with the death juice of as many tiny creatures as possible. It is felt by many cats that the continuing marketing of Litebeer encapsulates humans' overall failure to understand a fundamental fact of feline nature: that cats are animals of extremes, unwilling to accept the middle-ground and eternally fearful of the mediocre.

Satan's Coal
The one dried, blackened gribbly bit of food at the bottom of the food bowl that a cat will always leave behind, no matter how hungry it seems to be before (or after) feeding time. The legend of Satan's Coal, which hasn't got anything to do with coal whatsoever, goes all the way back to the time when Osiris, a farm cat in eighteenth-century Yorkshire, found a nugget of dried shrew corpse on the floor of a neighbour's barn that had been mysteriously ignored by whichever animal had caught it. So moggy folkore says, Osiris was 'dared' to eat the tempting nugget by a local witch's cat, and subsequently keeled over and died. Even

pragmatic, hardheaded cats who view the story of Satan's Coal as 'gobbledigook' often find themselves steering away from that last gribbly bit at feeding time, putting a paw to their stomach and offering such transparent excuses as 'I'm on the Catkins diet at the moment' and 'No, seriously, I'm podged – I found a smoky bacon-flavoured crisp on the floor earlier and, as you know, those things are surprisingly filling'.

Setting a Pissident
To urinate in a completely new and innovative place, instigating a trend for such action among your fellow felines. Born leaders but also kind of snotty, cats who set a pissident know that their originality comes at a price, and, upon seeing others follow lamely in their wake, can often be heard to mutter comments like 'Here come the mindless vultures, picking over the corpse of my brilliance' and 'Now I know how The Beatles must have felt when they heard the Marmalade's cover of "Ob-La-Di, Ob-La-Da".'

Waking up with Wood
To emerge, bleary eyed, from a nap and find a twig stuck to your tail that you didn't remember being there when you fell asleep.

Bewilderness

'Hi,' I said. 'I'm at the airport now, and I'm not feeling very good. I'll be on the plane soon, so I just wanted to say how much I love you, in case, well, you know, this is *it* – because I just have a feeling it might be.'

I clicked my mobile phone shut. It was a shame, I thought to myself, that the last time Dee would ever hear my voice would be via the medium of BT's 1571 answering service, but at least I had told her how I felt. It was important to express oneself, and many others who'd perished had not got the chance to. Feeling reassured, but not remotely calmed, by this, I felt nervously for the small plastic bottle of pills in my jacket pocket for the three hundredth time in the last hour, and headed back across Nairobi airport's departure lounge towards Zed, the photographer from *Jack* magazine.

'I think I might head back,' I told him.

'What? To the toilet? Again?' said Zed.

'No, I mean *back* back. Through customs.'

'What on earth are you talking about?'

'Well, you know, I'm not sure how confident I am about

doing this. I thought I might try to hire a car, go back that way instead.'

'Are you serious? You know how big Africa is, right?'

By the time I reached my mid-twenties, I had established a considerable pedigree as a bad traveller. Nonetheless, my trip to Kenya in the summer of 2002 was a new frontier even for someone as chronically poor at going on holiday as me: a work trip that I had ended up on by accident.

All the details were correct: I'd got the right plane, ended up in the right destination, met the appropriate people, and had not at any point in the process been mistaken for a different, globetrotting-adept Tom Cox, but that I was there at all surprised nobody as much as me.

I'd not so much been sent to Nairobi as bludgeoned there with flattery by an editor called James Brown, best known for founding the men's magazine *Loaded* in the early 1990s. Brown had just launched his new publication, *Jack* – a kind of *Loaded* for grown-ups, with the emphasis more on great outdoors adventure than nudity – and had telephoned me to offer me work after reading my first book.

'It's bloody brilliant!' he'd enthused. 'You could be our star feature writer.' I'd heard about Brown before, and witnessed fellow writers' and photographers' impersonations of him. They always seemed to make his voice more high-pitched than it really was, and you could see why: because of his zest for life. When you thought back to something he'd told you, there was a tendency to furnish it with an extra squeak.

Soon, I would get used to the capriciousness of Brown's enthusiasm. He was the kind of man who would phone you one day, out of the blue, and shout, 'I want you to go and learn falconry. It's going to be fucking wicked!' and then forget all about it the following morning. After I'd come back from Kenya – by plane – everyone I'd told about how I'd almost fled from the airport and driven a hire car back through Africa and Europe had thought I was barking mad, apart from Brown. 'Oh, bloody hell, why didn't you do it?' he'd said. 'It would have been fucking brilliant! A proper gonzo adventure! We could have run it as a serial!' A few months later, he would send me to participate in an erotic drawing class for another *Jack* feature, then, after seeing my rude, rudimentary sketches, call me, virtually foaming at the mouth, from his mobile phone, explaining that he was about to recommend that his friend, the well-known art dealer Jay Jopling, exhibit them in his gallery, White Cube.

'Yeah, right,' I said. '*Of course* you are.' But he insisted they were 'fucking brilliant' and 'like the work of a child savant'. I heard nothing else for a week, then cautiously mentioned the subject to him again.

'Oh yeah, them,' he'd said, and immediately changed the subject to his latest wild idea: something to do with releasing a lion into Trafalgar Square, as I remember.

However, in July 2002, all I knew was that Brown had a refreshingly unguarded passion for his job like that of nobody I'd ever worked for. Previously, if I'd kept a newspaper or magazine editor on the phone for more than four minutes, I'd worried that I was taking up far too much of the time of someone much more important than me. But Brown kept *me* on the phone for three quarters of an hour, talking about the Safari Rally, in which cars whizzed through the Kenyan countryside past lions and giraffes, and about his vision for *Jack*. 'Do you like cars?' he asked. 'Of course you do!' he continued before I had chance to admit that my interest in them didn't really get much more involved than enjoying early 70s cinema car chases featuring Ford Mustangs and Dodge Challengers. 'Everyone likes cars!' Somewhere in the midst of this dust storm of commissioning zeal, Brown had also mentioned that I would probably get the chance to meet a cheetah. At which point, I became quite a lot more interested.

There was just one hitch. Four years earlier, I had been on a plane that had been struck by lightning over the English Channel on the way back from Pisa. I am told by more experienced flyers that this happens relatively frequently and is generally not a great cause for concern, but I wouldn't have believed it at the time. When the lightning hit, a large blue flash had whizzed around the inside of the plane, many of the passengers had screamed, and there was speculation afterwards that the plane had dropped in the region of a thousand feet before righting itself. Back on terra firma, I made a decision: I had cheated aeronautical death, and I would not give it the chance to get its own back at a later date.

It's not that I didn't know the statistics about how rare aeroplane crashes were; I just knew that I didn't want to be in an aeroplane, thinking about having an aeroplane crash. To me, hearing the words 'I'm afraid it's terminal' with a number after them from a kindly person redirecting you at an airport was barely less ominous than hearing them as a stand-alone sentence in a hospital.

I was aware that ultimately the greater control I felt I had when I was travelling in a car or a train or a boat was an illusion, but it was an illusion that I cherished. Besides that, flying contradicted a fundamental belief of mine that it was against the laws of nature for any human to rise more than twenty storeys above ground level. Not long before I spoke to Brown, I'd been up to the first platform of the Eiffel Tower, and only just restrained myself from falling into a protective, terrified crawl in front of more insouciant sightseers. With this in mind, it is a tribute to his persuasive powers that during the course of our phone call he reduced my stance on flying from 'Never again!' to 'Maybe again, if someone carries on being complimentary about my work and talking about leopards for long enough!'

'Look at me,' boasted Brown. 'I've been up in fighter jets and skydived, and I'm all right. Take some valium. You'll be *fine*.'

Following Brown's advice, I did take some valium in the departure lounge at Heathrow. It calmed me down, but not enough to prevent me from leaving the first of two 'last goodbye' messages on the voicemail of Dee's mobile phone shortly before take-off. I then took some more valium, just to be sure. I noticed just a slight lessening of the certainty that my limbs would shortly be spread across the Alps in small pieces, but mostly I just wanted to go for a wee a lot. I tried to watch a couple of rom-coms on the screen in front of me and reread the same page of my book forty times, never taking a word of it in, then finally settled on a form of entertainment I found far more riveting than either: the virtual flight map, on which passengers could watch the plane move in barely perceptible increments across Europe and Africa. For me, this was more viscerally stimulating than the most explosive Bruce Willis movie. For the next eleven hours my eyes never left it, with the exception of the moments when I rushed to the bathroom, at one point knocking over the curry of Zed, *Jack's* photographer, in the process.

Having touched down in Nairobi and ventured out into its surrounding countryside, one of the first things to strike me was the special kind of dark it was subject to. It wasn't exactly that it was darker than the dark you found in rural England, just that it was more businesslike about getting down to it. They say that in Kenya, in July, they simply don't *do* dusk. 'But how can that be?' you think upon being first told this. 'It's not like part of the globe spins more quickly here than anywhere else, is it?' But then you experience it for yourself, and you realise the sun plummets to earth there at a different rate. It's like being part of a three-dimensional screen wipe. One moment the picture is there in front of your eyes: a heat haze, the dust cloud of a distant speeding car, a scattering of acacia trees, a couple of ostriches, the distant shadow of Mount Kilimanjaro. The next moment, it's eliminated by a blanket of black, the giant sleeping bag of the world abruptly zipped up in front of your face.

When you're part of a top rally crew, it's doubly important to pack up quickly when dark falls, since it won't be long before the hyenas and lions come down from the hills. As Paul, the gruff Yorkshireman responsible for leading the Subaru team for the 2002 Safari Rally, told me, there were also the Maasai tribesmen to contend with, who had been known to pilfer parts of the cars as souvenirs. 'You have to remember these people don't understand modern life,' he said. 'They don't have a mortgage or a pension plan.' He pointed this out as if he viewed it as a shortcoming:

something they needed to think about, if they were going to stop faffing about and get ahead in the world.

Not being part of a top rally crew myself, and being much more keen on observing hyenas and lions than rally, I couldn't say I had a vested interest in getting tidied up quickly. Actually, I might have been tempted to slow the process down by hiding a front coilover or a couple of torsion mounts belonging to one of the cars, had I been a bit braver, or had the faintest idea what they were. As for the Maasai, I'd been wandering around the test course for the Subaru team for a couple of days, and I'd met quite a few of them. All had been extremely personable, and surprisingly knowledgable about Subaru's stars. The most memorable included Jonathan and David, two twentysomethings with stretched earlobes and shukas who said that during the Safari they thought nothing of walking thirty miles to find out the results, and the patrician Father John, who enthused to me about the handbrake action of Subaru's best-known driver, Tommi Makinen. These men were additionally notable for each pulling behind them cows bearing a remarkable resemblance to the jazz musician and raconteur George Melly.

Sadly, the Maasai's enthusiasm for foreign culture did not appear to be reciprocated by the members of the rally team, to most of whom they seemed invisible at best and a nuisance at worst. Only Stuart, a half-deaf Welshman responsible for technical work on the cars, talked of the Maasai fondly, recalling the time a few years earlier when, twenty miles from the nearest village, as night raced out of the sky, he was forced to push a tyre truck out of black cotton mud and felt an ice-cold hand on his shoulder.

'I turned around and staring me in the face was this

great massive Maasai done up in the full Adam Ant outfit!'
he remembered. 'War paint, the lot. He just looked at me
and said, "Would you like a hand, old chap?"' I liked Stuart
instantly, which was lucky, since later that day, he would
be responsible for my safety, driving me along everyday
roads back to Nairobi at speeds of almost 200kph in the
Subaru Impreza WRC2002 normally driven by Petter
Solberg.

'You're not going to go *quite* that fast, are you?' I asked
him.

'Yup.' He flicked a mosquito off his arm, and I sensed the
insect served as a metaphor for my question. 'The only way
these things are designed to be driven is flat.'

'Flat' was what the Subaru team said when they meant
'flat out'. As I was learning, in the fast-moving world of
rally, cutting out one minuscule word could make the crucial difference between victory and defeat.

I didn't wish to appear fussy, but I couldn't help raising
another issue that was weighing heavily on my mind. 'But
aren't you worried we might hit a cow?' I said.

'I wouldn't worry,' he said, pointing to the car. 'These
things can stop on a sixpence.'

But I hadn't seen any sixpences on the route from
Nairobi, just Maasai, livestock, spluttering 1970s Toyotas,
and a series of terrifying spikes in the road, installed every
couple of miles as a primeval speed deterrent. I also knew
that, despite what Stuart had said, cows in fact *were* a concern, since, when I'd mentioned them to Tommi Makinen,
he'd called them an 'obvious danger'.

I'd looked at Makinen in sympathy at the time, thinking
how gut-wrenching it would be to be responsible for the
death of such an innocent, big-eyed creature: the terrible

flashbacks and inevitable months of emotional limping that would follow.

'Yep,' Makinen had then added. 'They can do some serious damage to a car.'

There are a couple of things people tend to be surprised at when I tell them about my trip to Africa. One is that when I was finally in the rally car, I was far more scared about the prospect of flying home than I was about hurtling along an ordinary road, with little visibility, at almost two hundred kilometres per hour. The other is that when I arrived at the test run site the morning after the flight, one of the first things I decided to do was chase two ostriches.

The ostriches in question were pecking away on the plains about a mile away from where the Subaru team worked on the cars. By this point, I'd already watched Solberg's first test run. It had been a brief, spectacular sight: the car shooting away into the hills in a cloud of dust, and disappearing until only the distant, angry wasp sound of its engine remained. The eternally seven-year-old, Scalextric-playing part of me had experienced a small tingle up the spine, but in the end, what I was watching was a fast car, and like other fast cars, its wheels moved, it made a noise, then it wasn't there any more. For me, this made the excitement of the experience limited. What was less limited was the excitement that behind any bush could be lurking creatures I'd only ever before seen at the zoo and on wildlife documentaries.

Not long after I returned from Kenya, I watched one of those documentaries, in which the narrator pointed out that 'ostriches can lash out and kill a cheetah with a deadly kick'.

Strangely, this had not occurred to me while I was looking at some ostriches in the flesh, and trying to persuade them to be my friends. Perhaps it was that I was still under the sway of the valium, which, while not particularly great at stopping a person from worrying about being swallowed up in a fireball of burning metal, was evidently fantastic at stopping them from worrying about being trampled into human risotto by a big, sod-off bird foot. I can also say that, while the two ostriches might have stood their ground in the face of a cheetah attack, they were absolutely petrified of me. Each time I picked up my pace and gained on them, they moved a little further away, until, finally, feeling a bit like a swimmer lost in the rhythm of the waves who suddenly looks back at the shore and can't remember which part of the beach he left his towel on, I gave up the ghost and turned back.

This began a pattern that would continue for the next three and a half days: brief bursts of animation from the rally crew, followed by long periods of waiting around, in which I tried to amuse myself by venturing off, sometimes accompanied by Zed, but mostly alone, in search of wildlife. Back in the United Kingdom, I'd been cautious enough about heading through a gently disreputable area of Norwich at night, but out here, in the middle of nowhere, surrounded by tribesman and large, hungry animals, I felt unconcerned. Managing the impossible feat of surviving 4,238 miles at a height at which no human should rightly travel had made me briefly invincible. After that, nothing could touch me.

On the second day, having tracked what I thought was a warthog but was actually an undersized mule, I found myself alone, in a clearing, with a lone dark figure walking towards me, holding a spear in one hand and a black rectangular object in the other. Had he skewered me, taken my wallet, and left me for dead, neither Zed nor the Subaru team would have been able to hear me scream. Preoccupied with their front coilovers and torsion mounts, it would only have been three or four hours later, at night's violent, decisive fall, that they would have remembered that guy in the corduroy flares who seemed so indifferent to the cars and weirdly interested in the animals. By then, it would have been too dark for the helicopter to find me.

As it was, the figure – another Maasai – greeted me with a handshake.

'Subaru?' he asked, showing me a mouth full of well-meaning teeth.

I nodded yes, even though I had an instinct to disassociate myself from the brand. I could have told him that, had he come to Norfolk, and been cut up by one of the county's many Impreza drivers on the stretch of the A11 yet to be transformed into a dual carriageway, his rose-tinted vision of the vehicle would soon be muddied, but what kind of crucifier of fun would that have made me?

As the Maasai had got closer to me, I'd realised that the object in his non-spear hand was a boombox. I recognised the tune playing as 'The Eye of the Tiger' by Survivor, made famous by the movie *Rocky III*.

This was not the right continent for tigers, of course, but I had my hopes of seeing a lion. In retrospect, I hadn't really thought through how this would transpire. I suppose I imagined I would just happen across one from just the perfect distance: not so close that it would have an instant instinct to bite my chin off, but close enough to get a good view, and a photograph to prove it.

In truth, Brown had somewhat exaggerated the element of intermingling between rally folk and animals. 'There are lions and ostriches and rhinos getting out the way of the car and everything! It's fucking wicked!' he said. While a car had once heartbreakingly hit a giraffe during a practice run, many years earlier, now a helicopter zoomed ahead of the cars, preventing further similar mishaps. I also found out that the 'personable' cheetah that I'd seen posed in photos with members of the Subaru team had actually been sedated for the purposes of the shoot.

'What is the worst experience you've had on a rally here?' I asked Makinen.

'Oh. One time, one of those big birds smashed the windscreen,' he said.

'What? Gosh. You mean an ostrich?'

'No. Like a chicken. You know.' He spread his arms as fully as he could. I had never seen a chicken even half that wide, and felt it was imperative that, before I headed home the following day, I made an effort to track one down.

When my article about my time with the Subaru team was published in *Jack*, it was accompanied by a photograph of one of the Imprezas skidding through a cloud of dust. Beneath it was another, of a giraffe, strolling innocently along what could potentially be a track carved out through the dirt for rally cars. 'Danger on the dirt,' read a caption connecting the two photographs. '200km/hour Subaru Impreza shares the same route with pedestrian 1900kg adult male giraffe!' In actuality, the giraffe in question was nowhere near the rally route at all, but safely sequestered in Nairobi National Park, where the greatest automotive danger it faced was a Renault

Espace, being driven by a rotund, jocular Kenyan man called Maurice, who was carefully observing a sign reading 'Speed Limit 20KPH: Warthogs and Children Have Right of Way'.

As if to underline the rally stars' emotionally detached relationship to the wildlife around them, they had been known to eat at The Carnivore, a restaurant specialising in the meat of many of the animals they might potentially run over.

At The Carnivore, a different waiter was assigned to each different kind of game, which they carried from the grill on large swords. I didn't know if they got commission on the meat they offloaded, but the system did appear to bring a competitive element to proceedings, making the restaurant a sort of inadvertent afterlife version of the battles the animals in question fought daily on the Serengeti. On my visit there, I was invited to eat an unlimited supply of hartebeest, zebra, crocodile, waterbuck and impala, and reluctantly obliged. I felt particularly sorry for the waiter assigned to waterbuck, who was having some wretched luck.

The waiter's sales technique didn't involve anything more elaborate than saying 'Waterbuck?' to each table he approached, but in those three syllables, an ocean of hurt was conveyed. You might think that a man saying 'Waterbuck?' is just a man asking if you want some waterbuck, but in truth, there are lots of different ways of saying 'Waterbuck?': there's the 'Waterbuck?' that says 'Are you hungry? Would you like some of this?', the 'Waterbuck?' that says 'I have a wife and four kids to support, and the carburettor has just messed up on my 1981 Mazda', the 'Waterbuck?' that says 'this is an extremely big sword, and has many other potential uses, besides its function as a meat carrying apparatus'. And then there is the '*Waterbuck?*' that quite simply says, 'I am dying inside: rescue me'.

I wanted to help, but I was already feeling a bit queasy. That night, in my hotel room, suffering from the Meat Sweats, I felt the ache of the traitor coming from deep in my abdomen. I was not a vegetarian, and the meat I had eaten could hardly have been more free range, but by eating it, I had gone over to the side of the enemy, betrayed the animals I had tentatively aligned myself with. If I had actually enjoyed it, it might not have been so bad. The zebra had been dry, and tasted suspiciously what I imagined horse might taste like, the hartebeest left no lasting impression in my mind and, while I would never have admitted it to its face, the crocodile had only been passable. As for the waterbuck, the less said about that the better. I could only assume that, before its unfortunate demise, it had been an unusually sedentary kind of antelope.

With Maurice's help, I did see my lions in the end: two females, basking in the morning sun a matter of four or five yards away in the road in front of the Espace. Standing up with my head and shoulders sticking out of the sunroof, I was an easy target. A couple of relatively languid movements of their powerful limbs, and they would have had a hearty corduroy-flavoured breakfast. This was a National Park, a controlled environment, not the 'real' wilderness surrounding the rally track, but it was still a brave move, by my standards. You could say the same about my bumpy, skidding attempt to traverse the same rally route that the Subarus did, in a Range Rover, in record time, or the moment later that day when, following an engine failure, I was left to guard the abandoned spotter helicopter alone, putting my arm protectively around its chrome tail as thirty

intrigued Maasai encroached, and appeasing them by handing out water and fruit that I'd found in the cockpit. I had
my mind on bigger things. Specifically, one significantly
bigger thing that, by some sort of Satanic magic that I
neither understood nor wished to understand, would be
transporting me back to the UK later that evening.

Since then, I've had plenty of opportunities to get on planes,
and have turned every one of them down. Required to go to
Spain or the south of France for two days of work, I have
opted to spend the same amount of time travelling there
and back on a sleeper train, cramped in airless compartments
with wittering, text message-happy lovebird students, in pref-
erence to two flights each lasting not much longer than a
particularly indulgent bath. In all honesty, it does not bother
me unduly that I have never ticked the travelling boxes of
the conventionally worldly person. I am happy to read
others' experiences of rain forests, pyramids and hanging gardens. What does concern me more is the animal life I am
missing out on. Because of my flying phobia, I might never
get the chance to feed an ice cream to a capybara or have my
hat stolen by lemur, and that, quite honestly, rankles.

'I want you to go to Tasmania and track the Tasmanian
devil!' enthused Brown a few weeks after my return from
Kenya. I considered the offer for a day or two, and did a bit
of research about Tasmanian devils, learning that they were
the world's biggest carnivorous marsupial, 'characterised by
their black fur, pungent odour when stressed, extremely loud
and disturbing screech and ferocity while feeding', and were
teetering close to the endangered list due to the horrific-
sounding 'devil face tumour disease'. I was very taken with

the photographs of them – or at least those that didn't show-case devil face tumours – but then I realised the flying time from London to Tasmania was twenty-four hours and thirty-five minutes, and thought back to a montage of images from my flight home from Kenya: me sitting in the departure lounge, overdoing the valium slightly again and phoning Dee with another tearful farewell-forever speech, the plane shooting up, up, up into the night sky for so long I worried that the pilot had forgotten to follow the curve of the globe and decided to head straight for the ice planet Hoth instead . . . me searching for any sort of remedy for calm, and only finding it in vague form in the sound of Neil Young's 'Harvest' on the in-flight headphones. I knew that, if I probed, and committed, somewhere deep within I might find the gonzo travel writer Brown was grooming me to be, and that it was all about the power of self-belief: whatever a person chose to most believe about himself, more than likely was what he would be. That was all very well, but unfortunately what I most believed about myself was that I was a big landlocked chicken whose bowels could turn to concrete at the mere sight of a duty-free shop.

I found some solace in the knowledge that, had I gone to Tasmania, it was highly unlikely I would have been able to engage with a Tasmanian devil in a meaningful way. Also, it wasn't exactly as if I struggled to find other animals that were characterised by their black fur, pungent odour when stressed, extremely loud and disturbing screech and ferocity while feeding in my nearby vicinity. If I squinted when I looked at The Bear while he was yawning, I could even pre-tend I was in Tasmania, facing down the devil himself.

I suppose I'm lucky in this way: I don't necessarily find so-called 'mundane' animals any less interesting than wild or endangered ones. I certainly enjoy seeing the cheetahs and maned wolves at my local zoo, but they just don't have the same potential for interaction as you get with The People Sheep and the unruly local gang of pot-bellied pygmy goats[6] who like to put their hooves up on my chest and bully me for nuts. Nine times out of ten, I will opt for stroking the velvety muzzle of a donkey over admiring a Bactrian camel from afar or getting into a staring contest with a supercilious elf owl. Obviously, the buzz that comes from the danger of being in close quarters to a larger, more aggressive animal is a favourable factor, but if I need my big-cat fix, I can always use my imagination and press my head really low to the ground while Shipley is padding across the living room carpet, or stare at a puncture wound Ralph has given me on my finger in one of his more overzealous moments and pretend the digit in question is a tiny, limbless person called Edward. That said, when, in early 2009, my cat behaviourist friend Vicky asked me if I wanted to go to Kent and put my hand inside a tiger's mouth, I did not prevaricate before saying yes.

It was probably a measure of how long it had been since I'd been close to big cats, and how little I knew about the way a person must act around them, that when Vicky invited me to come with her to the Wildlife Heritage Foundation, near Ashford, I assumed that I'd be behind the bars with them, possibly having a little cuddle as I fed them. Looking back, I'm surprised by how calm I was about this prospect, especially as Vicky had told me that the tiger she was working with, Ronja, had been rescued from an Eastern European circus, where her leg had been injured,

---

[6] I don't believe the pot-bellied pygmy goat is an actual breed; these are just pygmy goats who eat a bit too much.

and was bad-tempered and stressed as a result. I suppose it might be put down to the significant existential turning point I had come to at the time. The major relationship of my life was ending, and I was viewing my situation philosophically. I'd been on the planet for thirty-three years, been lucky enough to spend eight and a half of them with an intelligent, beautiful woman, fulfilled a lot of my working goals, and I could think of far more dismal, less apt ways to exit this mortal coil than by being crushed between giant, feline jaws.

Vicky told no word of a lie: I think I did put my hand in a tiger's mouth, for about 0.3 of a second, but there were metal bars offering a certain amount of protection, and I can't say for sure exactly where hand, mouth and proffered chicken drumstick intersected. The tiger concerned was not Ronja, who refused to come near me, but a smaller female called Indy. This could be viewed as a cop-out, but would no doubt come in useful as an anecdote to wheel out the next time someone mocked me for being nervous about feeding apples to horses. Five minutes earlier, I'd done something similar with a snow leopard: a magnificent, draught excluder-tailed creature who put my frequent boasting to friends about the size of Ralph's paws sharply into perspective.

Next, it was on to the Pallas cats, which were a far more manageable size. In fact, with the exception of their unusual pointy ears and round pupils, they looked not entirely unlike domestic tabbies. That said, they would clearly be more than happy to mess you up, given half the opportunity. Seeing one blink at me, I automatically reverted to the high-low whistle I used to get my cats to come to me, then checked no manly keepers were around, before punctuating it with a small, ineffectual kissy noise.

'What are you doing?' asked Vicky.

'I don't know,' I said. 'It just seemed right.'

'Somehow I don't think that's a language it will understand.'

I could see her point, and I could see the male Pallas cat's point too. Who did I think I was, after all, bringing my soppy white middle-class cat owner ways into this virtual jungle, whose residents would sooner tear up a Cosipet Cat Igloo with their teeth than curl up in one? I knew what the Pallas was driving at, but it didn't need to be quite so damning with its scowl. Sure, it was very easy on the eye, but it had its defects, too. There was the hair, for a start, which was positively crying out for a bit of product. I'm not the kind of individual who likes to bathe and groom his cats, but I had to admit I would have relished five minutes on a pelt like this with a VO5 hot oil treatment and a bottle of Kiehl's Silk Groom.

In the movement of the cats Vicky introduced me to, I could frequently see the swagger of my own moggies writ large. Tigers, leopards and lions didn't meow, and Mark, the head keeper at the foundation, said that tigers were actually quite doglike in many ways, but each of these animals made a noise the keepers called 'chuffling', not unlike a purr. When Sarah, the keeper responsible for showing us around, called to the one resident cheetah, Mephisto, he made a chirruping sound not dissimilar to the one Ralph and Shipley's late brother Brewer used to make at mealtimes. These cats had the gender preferences so common to household felines, too. Ronja, just like Bootsy, was more drawn to women, and had even taken against a keeper called Fraser when he had cut off his long, girlish blond hair. Ronja, in her playful moments, had a Shipley-like habit of ripping up books, except her particular taste ran less to John Irving novels and more to telephone directories.

Perhaps most amazingly, in the work she had been doing for the WHF, Vicky had been plying Ronja with extra-strength catnip and seeing impressively playful results. When Vicky starts talking about catnip, it seems somehow wrong that she's walking about in broad daylight with no protective goons around her, and not mooching about in a sinister fashion in a silk dressing gown, in some fiercely secretive underground lair, with her own very expensive set of personalised scales. She knows her stuff. She'd recommended a couple of incredibly potent brands to me in the past, one of which sent Bootsy and Pablo into such a state of free-love rapture, I felt sure one of them was about to stagger blearily over to the shelves where I kept my LPs and roll some of the substance in question up on the sleeve of Cream's *Disraeli Gears* album, and another which, at the height of its potency, had convinced Ralph that he could lay waste to a four-foot-high antique chest of drawers. But Vicky assured me that the uncut stuff she was using on her biggest client was something else entirely: the kind of thing that, after one whiff, could take the head clean off a normal house cat.

Around the time of my visit to the Wildlife Heritage Foundation, a video had been doing the rounds on the Internet featuring Christian, a lion cub purchased by two well-spoken hippies, John Rendall and Ace Berg, from the famous Knightsbridge store Harrods in 1969, and raised in their London flat. The main clip, which I'd receive a link in my inbox to around three times a day on average at the time, showed an emotional reunion between John, Ace and a fully grown Christian in the African wilderness, a year after they'd released him. By that point, Christian had become head of his own pride, and John and Ace had been assured he would not remember them. The unalloyed delight on their faces as he ran across the scrubby land and into their arms was real, icy-tingle-down-the-spine stuff, the kind of thing you'd have to be made out of reinforced steel not to be moved by. No matter what rousing musical crescendo it was set to on YouTube, it had the same power, and provoked astonished questions from millions of animal lovers, chief among them being, 'How can a wild animal love its guardians so deeply?' and, 'No sodding way! You actually used to be able to buy lions in Harrods?'

Over the ensuing weeks, more images of Christian had been heavily circulated. Christian in the grounds of a London church, where a vicar had kindly allowed John and Ace to exercise him; Christian on the sofa with John and Ace; Christian with his paws up on an old black-and-white television and a 'Who? Me? What? I didn't do nuffin'!' look on his face. As someone who spent much of his time living in his own unrealistically edited version of 1969, I found it an enormously appealing fantasy, and, heading back to a house hosting only cats, I wondered if, at this somewhat pivotal moment in my life, it could be The Answer. Me and another side-burned, corduroy-wearing friend, taking up together in easygoing bachelordom, raising our own big cat; our reputation for kindness, iconoclasm and daring growing bigger with each week; the inevitable legendary parties and *Elle Decoration* magazine cover shoot that would follow.

But then I thought back to the lions at WHF. As Sarah the keeper had told me, there was currently a problem with them urinating in their drinking trough. My next-door neighbours

Deborah and David had recently worked hard to dig out a new pond in their garden, so I could see some potential issues there. I suppose I could rule out tigers, for similar reasons, having witnessed the power of their spraying at fairly close quarters. I also thought of that one grumpy-looking male lion who Sarah had told me had had a fight with a rival, and suffered a claw through the testicle, only just avoiding castration. I'd witnessed some raw scenes in my vet's waiting room, but I wondered if this would be a step too far.

A Pallas cat was more manageable, but would I really fancy trying to get one into a cat basket? Perhaps most enticing of all was Artem, the snow leopard I'd fed, who would without question look great on Ralph's favourite sheepskin rug. By adopting one of his future cubs, I could avoid being accused of plagiarising Ace and John.

But one WHF snow leopard had recently had to have part of his bowels removed, having eaten an unusually tough bit of horse's mane by mistake. The corpse-filled shed it had come from, which Vicky and Sarah had given me a fetid peek into, seemed to be an essential part of big-cat ownership, and I didn't have room to erect such a thing in my garden. It had been hard enough watching an ill Janet slinking around the place recently, and I wasn't sure I could really deal with a grouchy snow leopard slumped in the corner of the room complaining about stomach pains. I'm sure there would be good times to offset it, but I didn't need that sort of emotional rollercoaster right now. Ultimately, it would not make life better, only more complicated. Besides, big-cat ownership just wasn't very 'me'. This, anyway, is what I tried to convince myself, as I made the long, safe drive back to the place I'd come to call home.

'Has That Cat Just Sniffed Some Spottle, or Is It Just Pleased to See Me?': A Guide to Four Underacknowledged Types of Cat Dirt

Fruzz

Many cat owners spend literally hours puzzling how, in the course of one small tussle with a fellow member of its species or an energetic cleaning session, a feline can shed what appears to be its entire body weight in fur yet appear more or less physically unchanged. The answer lies with fruzz: a miraculous expanding substance often mistaken for 'fluff' and the other less intriguing, hair-related waste produced by more pedestrian animals. Fruzz cannot be truly categorised as Fruzz until it has left the surface of the cat in question, at which point it immediately begins to grow at a rate both violent and imperceptible. This means it is incredibly hard to describe to those who've never come into direct contact with it. You can instruct them to picture a protein filament version of a just-add-water instant pudding, but even then you're only scratching the surface of its true nature.

Fruzz is far from the most unpleasant kind of cat filth, and environmental scientists believe it has hitherto untapped potential for recycling[7], but complacency about its existence remains one of the most frequent reasons that moggy slaves tend to underestimate when budgeting for electronic cleaning devices. It is also one of the major unacknowledged elements that separate cat owners from normal civilians in embarrassing ways. This is evinced by conversations such as the following:

Cat owner (fondling Miele Aquarius S5580): 'So, how does this baby perform when it comes to fruzz?'

Vacuum cleaner salesman: 'Mr Babbidge, can you call security, please? I think we've got one of those people from the special hospital in the shop again!'

Crunk

A dangerously adhesive, bitty, saliva-like substance not dissimilar to regurgitated digestive biscuits. Manufactured in an alarmingly large range of colours including Devil's Night Black, Off Grey and – most popular of all – Carrot Vomit Orange, crunk is most often found on cats' chins and

---

[7] See the ever-popular 'Fruzz Bird' – for which you will need the following ingredients:
1. A rubber-dimpled pet mitt.
2. A cat.
3. A light breeze.
4. An open first-storey – or higher – window.
5. Some fruzz.

surrounding areas. Much murky confusion surrounds this enigmatic cat detritus, especially in the case of those unfortunate souls who have been known to mistake it for the energy drink of the same name pioneered by the Atlanta-based rapper Lil Jon.

The first genuinely disturbing crunk moment often comes when, having assumed that what you're dealing with is mere spit, the realisation dawns that it is, in fact, crunk, and any resemblance between the colour of it and your cat's fur is mere coincidence. The second comes about two minutes later when, having turned your back on said feline for a matter of seconds while searching for some kitchen roll, you realise that the crunk has vanished. In one way, this is good news. Any cat without crunk on its chin is a more pleasant cat to be around! In another way, it is the worst news possible: you can bet your bottom dollar that that crunk didn't just disappear into thin air, and its final destination will be a mystery guaranteed to haunt your very soul into the midnight hour and beyond.

Mair
While the phrase 'I've had a "mare"' does not signify anything pleasant when uttered by a normal citizen, it always gives rise to an extra shiver among cat owners. Nightmares are one thing, but walking into a kitchen in the stark light of day and finding beloved woks, floors, bowls – woks, floors and bowls that you'd scrubbed to within an inch of your life – flecked liberally with mair is another entirely.

Those who've accidentally rested their hand on a shag-pile rug or a passing donkey after using Pritt Stick will have a generalised idea about mair's fuzzy, sticky horror. But at least with Pritt Stick and a donkey, you know where you are.

With mair, you're always on your toes (although thankfully not literally, since that would *truly* be a sod to remove). 'Is the sticky bit in the middle regurgitated wet cat food, or some of last night's sticky toffee pudding that Janet accidentally got caught in his tail while illegally roaming the kitchen counter?' I might ask myself, as I examine some mair. And while you tend to assume that the hairy coating on the outside of the mair in question comes from one of the cats themselves, who's to say it isn't actually the product of a vole they killed last night, or a combination of both?

A particular liability to habitual finger-lickers, mair can, with a little effort, usually be removed from skin – one of the stronger types of hand wash associated with the medical profession will normally do the trick. The problem is as much one of 'When?' as it is one of 'How?' Do you clean your hands now, or when you've finished sitting on the kitchen floor, crying, and fantasising about a world where there isn't always at least five cat dishes stained with gribbly bits in your immediate eye line? Do you do it before you've started drying that painstakingly de-maired bowl, with that tea towel that might have more mair on it, or afterwards? And even when that's done, there are the fixed objects around you to think about. Those surfaces might look clean from a distance, but look again. It is a rare occasion, worth celebrating, when a cat owner's kitchen doesn't showcase at least one cupboard with a strip of mair stuck to it.

Spottle
'Like Wee, but Even More Long-Lasting and Orange!' might not seem like the most irresistible marketing slogan to most of us, but those who use spottle to disorientate and subjugate their minions will no doubt disagree. Unlike a cat that has

flagrantly and expansively urinated on, say, a curtain or a particularly irritating section of skirting board, the spottling cat cannot be so easily singled out as an offender. This is not to say his aim is any less deadly. Quite the contrary: spottling is such a fine art, it has even led some humans to speculate whether their cats have tiny little paint brushes concealed beneath their tails.

'Did that cat just spottle?' you will often find yourself asking, as the culprit gently shimmies backwards into a corner of the living room. 'Or is he just unusually fond of our new lava lamp?' Since it can take up to five hours for spottle's virulent, mocking hues to fully materialise, laying blame is rendered harder still. By the time you've concluded that, yes, your cat did spottle on the cover of Richard Russo's Pulitzer prize-winning 2001 novel, *Empire Falls*, the culprit is long gone, lazing happily somewhere beneath a fig tree in the garden or spottling on the freshly unwrapped packaging of next door's new petrol-powered strimmer. Some spottle, in fact, remains invisible forever, and in such cases the only way to detect it is to insert another cat nose first into the suspected area. If the cat looks up from the spot in question with its mouth half-open and a slightly deranged expression on its face, not unlike that of Anthony Hopkins when he smells something that awakes a bad part of him in *Silence of the Lambs*, you know that you're dealing with spottle. Hence the well-known phrase: 'Is that some spottle that cat has just sniffed, or is it just not remotely pleased to see me?'

Walk This Way

Seven forty-five am is not a time I generally associate with my friend Simon. For someone like me, who works best in the earlier part of the day and has spent much of his life being woken up by a series of ever-more-insistent furry alarm clocks, that's virtually lunchtime, but Simon is an actor and, like many in his profession, he moves at a more controlled pace. Unless there's a shoot or a casting call to get up for, his day tends not to truly start until most normal people are leaving work and does not hit its full stride until last orders are announced. So when I heard him out in the garden, not long after the dawn chorus, loudly kissing his girlfriend, I was surprised.

The party the night before had been a lively one: my first, for almost nine years, as a single person. Simon, one of my regular golfing partners, had hosted it to coincide with the final round of the United States Masters tournament and, after the winner had been decided, the guests who were there to watch the golf and the guests who were there to stare disapprovingly at the guests who were there to watch the golf had set aside their differences and come together in raucous unison. My main fuzzy memory upon waking up in Simon's spare room had been the image of a hirsute, irrepressibly cheery man called John repeatedly hugging me, and shouting, 'You like music! And you're really thin!' while, across the room, Simon simultaneously held his girlfriend Kerry and her best friend upside down by their ankles.

Still, as good a time as I'd had, I could not help viewing proceedings through the prism of my recently acquired single status. Whether I was or was not technically in a room full of laughing couples in airtight relationships built to withstand the test of time was immaterial; it was inevitably going to feel that way. Hearing Simon kissing Kerry outside was just more evidence that not one other person in the entire universe was on their own. My guess was that the two of them were so utterly ensconced in each other, they hadn't been able to yet bear the pain of going to bed and being parted by sleep. Ideally, I would have liked to have gone down to the garden and seen if I could befriend one of the numerous neighbourhood cats who regularly drove Simon to distraction by soiling his freshly planted herb garden. But I had no wish to disturb a lovers' tryst, so kept away from the window, and sat for a while, rubbing my eyes and taking in my surroundings.

On the wall I could see promotional posters from a couple of the TV shows Simon had starred in, and an Edinburgh Festival stand-up gig from a few years earlier, but dominating the room were two giant wall charts, depicting popular breeds of dogs: one focusing on larger breeds, one on smaller. The age-old canine versus feline debate was one in which Simon and I had reached a grumbling impasse. Having grown up on a farm in Yorkshire, surrounded by spaniels, Simon quite simply didn't have time for cats' idle nonsense. For the first two years we'd known each other, the subject of my own moggy ownership hadn't come up, and when it had, he'd appraised me over his pint with a raised eyebrow, as if I had suddenly become a stranger to him. Since then, he'd learned to accept it, in the manner one might learn to accept someone who, while otherwise a regular kind of bloke, had a penchant for occasionally going out in public with a clutch purse. I knew it wasn't precisely what he was looking for in a friendship, but I sensed the way he viewed it was that, by your mid-thirties, we all had our baggage, and, as a result, one sometimes had to compromise.

My mouth was a bit dry, so, after a few minutes reorientating myself, I crept downstairs for a glass of water. I kept away from the window, in an attempt not to disturb Simon and Kerry, but, as I was turning away from the sink, I caught Simon's reflection in the glass, his arm gently and amorously offered. On the end of the arm I expected to see Kerry, but instead saw a small chunk of sausage, left over from the previous night's barbecue. And on the end of the sausage was a black and white cat of quite magnificent fluffiness.

'Morning,' I said, opening the back door.

'Oh,' he said. 'Er, morning.' He could not have looked more guilty if I'd caught him writing 'golf is shit' on a wall.

'I thought you didn't like them,' I said.

'Well, perhaps I went a bit far in saying I didn't like them. I'm just indifferent to them. I do like to say hello to them, though. I call this one Princess.'

'You have nicknames for them?'

'Yeah. That one's The General.' I looked up toward the garden fence of the house to the rear of Simon's, on top of which sat another cat, this time black and short-haired, observing us phlegmatically. 'There's also Whiskers, but she isn't here at the moment. She likes to wander more.'

I've known many men who profess to dislike cats, but a surprising amount of the same men, if pushed, will admit that they at least 'don't mind' them; the dislike is a masculine façade, like a workbench you keep clearly visible in your shed but don't intend to use. Simon, it seemed, could now be added to their ranks. For me, this was a relief – not just because it gave me a glimpse of an extra, unsuspected soft side to one of my best friends, but because, for the previous twenty-four hours, I had been experiencing a new kind of solitude in my status as a cat lover. Again and again, I had explained to Simon's friends that I owned six cats, and they had looked at me in bewilderment. 'Oh, right,' they'd said. 'How do you cope with the . . . hair and stuff?' As they narrowed their eyes, I could almost see myself reflected back in their pupils, changing shape until I morphed into a 74-year-old Polish widower at war with the local council over his hoarding habits and the mysterious tang emanating from his shed.

Of course, part of my feeling was just down to a rare set of circumstances: the fact that the people at this party, owing partly to the fact that Simon was a Dog Person and partly to sheer chance, happened to be exclusively cat-indifferent. Yet I was also aware that what I was feeling had a greater significance: that it was a part of a mutation I was undergoing, as an owner of cats.

After just over two months, I was finding that being single was not without its perks. I was now my own person, and I made my own decisions. Keen to take advantage of my situation to the full, throwing caution to the wind, I would sometimes throw a wet towel on the bathroom floor and

leave it there a whole four minutes before picking it up. But
in many other ways singleness was a bewildering phenomenon. I'd been single before, but since that had happened in
1647, it didn't provide any true frame of reference. 'What do
I want to do today?' I would ask myself on a free morning.
Or, upon watching a TV programme or picking up an item
of clothing in a shop, 'Remind me: what do I think of this,
again?' I would then experience the mystification of not
being able to come up with a satisfactory answer. There was
also the additional bewilderment that, the last time I was
single, I was not living alone with six cats.

I'd joked frequently about the slippery slope of cat ownership: my fears of becoming the sort of person who talks
about nothing but his cats, who can't tell that his house
smells strongly and off-puttingly of his cats because he's too
accustomed to the strong and off-putting smells his cats pro-
duce. But I'd never *really* thought of myself as having the
potential to be a Crazy Cat Man, or anything close, or even
that owning cats was 'my thing' any more than a handful of
my other main passions were 'my thing'. Had I never met
Dee, or another person who loved cats as much as Dee, I am
certain I would have never ended up with as many as six
cats. The cats were the product of our bond, and that bond
had provided a kind of social insulation for me. But I was
realising that owning six cats as a single person – whether
you be male or female – is different to owning six cats in a
long-term relationship. I wasn't ashamed of liking cats, and
Dee would soon be taking a couple of our moggies off my
hands, but I had to face the facts: the removal of one element had abruptly changed my domestic set-up from one
perceived as fairly normal to one that, in a certain light,
could be viewed as rather odd.

In the weeks following my split with Dee, I was told by cat-loving female friends that being a man who owns multiple felines marked me out as 'solid boyfriend material'. But, I reasoned, they *would* say that: they loved cats, and were being nice to me, because they were my friends, and knew I'd just been through arguably the major upheaval of my adult life. Their suggestion was that I was more 'sensitive' because I owned cats. But I was also aware that there was a flipside to the perception: that there are also women, even women who like cats, who will immediately start asking themselves questions about a man living alone with that many sets of paws. Why half a dozen – or even, as was looking to soon be the case, four – moggies and not just one? On a deeper level, what did the cats 'represent'? If I had that many animals, did it mean I couldn't relate to humans?

Were I to answer these questions, I would have said it was simple: I liked cats, my ex also liked cats, so we ended up getting a lot of cats, then, when we split up, due to practical reasons, I kept slightly more of the cats than her. But, as I knew all too well, that kind of explanation might not cut it in the real world.

Another single friend had recently signed up to one of the more wholesome Internet dating sites. She showed me her profile and asked me whether there was anything I thought she should add.

'You haven't mentioned that you like cats, have you?' I said.

'No,' she replied. 'That's because you don't. It's The Rule.' I noticed that in one of her photos she had cropped out Clive, her tabby. I felt sorry for Clive. Had he had any say in the matter?

'You wouldn't want to go out with someone who doesn't like cats, though, would you?' I asked her.

'No!' she replied, horrified.

I was a long way from even thinking about dating, but, if the time came, such was the minefield I might have to face. For the time being, I was having enough trouble dealing with the sheer logistics of living alone with six cats, never mind the social implications. A month or two after Simon's party, without assistance, I had taken them en masse to the vet to receive their annual booster jabs. I performed the task in two shifts, and, if you overlook the moment when Ralph sat on the examining table and ate a scab the vet had picked off his forehead, they went largely without incident. Even so, I could not shake the perception of myself as the eccentric master of some kind of miniature furry travelling circus.

Not long after that, a butch but ailing black stray turned up at my back door, looking up as I came to the window and beseechingly, almost ghoulishly, meowing at me. The stray did not let me near enough to stroke him but did let me near enough to see the cavernous open wound on his neck. For two minutes, before I collected myself, called at neighbours' houses to ascertain that it didn't belong to any of them, and telephoned the RSPCA, I descended into a squeamish panic, flailing around for answers in the space Dee used to occupy, the force of her absence suddenly so much more apparent. From then on, with the help of my neighbours, Deborah and David, who named the stray Winston, I kept a vigil, hearing his haunted-house mewling, sometimes spotting him, but not managing to lure him into our houses.

It was clear from the state of Winston's neck and his weeping eyes that if he didn't get treatment soon, he would not survive. The RSPCA paid us a visit, but could not find him, and left me with a cat trap of somewhat medieval appearance and a code number to give to my local vet when we caught Winston. On the fourth evening of our stakeout, Deborah and David and I set the trap on my patio. That night I kept my cats indoors: a task that I'd long ago decided was approximately as easy as containing Houdini in balsa wood. The six of them liked to give the impression that they got on one another's nerves, but when the occasion demanded it, they could happily work together, so I was surprised the next morning to find that they had not made a team effort to tunnel through the wall of the spare bedroom. Sadly, when I checked the trap, I found that it was Winston-free. I was also disappointed to have my secondary hope dashed: that, if Winston hadn't fallen for it, it might at least have now been playing host to a confused polecat who'd taken a wrong turn at the end of a heavy night. I proceeded to let Shipley, Janet, Ralph, The Bear, Bootsy and Pablo out. I then spent the rest of the day freeing each of them from the cat trap, as they took turns to sample its contents, which, despite containing exactly the same ingredients, were clearly far more interesting than the slap-up mechanically recovered meat feast they'd ignored first thing that morning.

Deborah, David and I continued to look for Winston that day beneath the foliage in our gardens, and came charging out of our bedrooms at the first sign of a foreign meow, to no avail, and again the following day, and for several days after that. I feared the worst, but I also hoped that, just maybe, another cat-lover in East Mendleham might have come to his rescue. He was a nervous cat, but his particular kind of nerves seemed to suggest a domestic past in recent memory, and it wasn't impossible that his owner might have found him.

When Deborah called to say he'd returned, it had been a fortnight since we'd seen him and we'd almost given up hope. I was in Norwich with friends at the time, and, though I rushed home, by the time I arrived Winston had vanished again, in the aftermath of his usual routine of pleading, meowing and affectionate patio rolling just out of arm's reach. But that night, using Deborah and David's supply of tinned salmon, we managed to lure him into the trap, and not long after dawn the following morning I rushed him to the emergency vet.

As I carried a hissing, pacing Winston through the house in the heavy trap, The Bear appeared as if by magic from one of his innumerable hiding places. His face could not have been more expressive if he'd found some white gloss and painted a fat question mark on it. I moved away from the trap a few steps towards The Bear, and stood halfway between the two of them: these two black cats, both of which had found me more than I'd found them, and who now seemed to bookend the most significant relationship of my life.

'Don't worry,' I told the uncaged one. 'We're at capacity already.' For once, I was not facing another test of pet owner's willpower: if Winston could not be re-homed, Deborah and David had said they would be willing to take him in.

I only left Winston in the entrance hall for five minutes, while I called the vet and put my jacket on, but his wound was so pungent that, four hours later, the room still reeked of it. However, I was assured by the vet that despite its horrific appearance, most of the damage had been caused by excessive scratching. A call the following day informed us that he was recovering well, and had been transferred to the RSPCA re-homing centre in Norwich.

It had been my first cat crisis as a single person. Amazingly, I had weathered it without crumpling into a ball and hiding under the stairs. But what if I experienced another crisis, involving one of my cats? Anything, it had occurred to me as I worried about Winston, could happen to Janet, Shipley, Pablo, Bootsy, The Bear or Ralph while I was out. Now, when I left the house, they would have nobody else to turn to in a time of trouble. And, as Winston proved, cats, despite their lone-gun hype, did need someone to turn to, sometimes. From this point on, when I left, I did so even more carefully than ever before, checking there was no flame on the hob, sometimes making one final journey back inside to 'say goodbye properly' to whichever cat happened to be around, and then one further final one, to switch the radio on.

'I suppose that's a security measure, is it?' my friend Will asked, as the two of us left the house for Norwich and I flicked a switch, filling the room with the hectoring sound of John Humphrys on the Radio Four *Today* programme.

'Yep,' I said. 'Got to keep the burglars away.' I was telling only a half-truth: for the gargantuan six hours I wasn't going to be around, I wanted to make sure the cats had some company.

It took some effort, but that July I finally did build up the courage to leave the cats for a few days. My trip was for work purposes, but I extended it in order to visit my friend Jackie in Wales. Jackie is an illustrator, and resides on the

Pembrokeshire coast in the kind of rural artist's paradise that makes any claim I've ever made to live 'in the middle of nowhere' seem like the deluded boasting of a jumped-up rural fantasist. While St David's, the closest town, has its share of tourists, Jackie's hamlet of Treleddyd Fawr is near-untouched by overflow; finding it, even by car, feels like a small explorer's victory. When, on my way back from it, I asked Jackie if she could recommend anywhere I could buy a nice sandwich 'nearby', she suggested a deli in Narberth which, at 23 miles away, she clearly perceived in the same way that many people perceive the newsagent at the end of their road.

To a more cynical, city-dwelling outsider, it might seem overblown when Jackie writes on her blog, 'Over the house this evening, a new moon, a copper bear and an ocean of air', 'In the high hill top ponies grazed and had cleared spaces beneath dry twisted trees' or of feeding her teenage children on nettles. But what becomes apparent upon visiting her ramshackle cottage, with its animal-shaped weather vanes and watercolour dragons, is that if everyone else lived here, they would talk like this too. It's the kind of place where having a conversation about whether a stuffed weasel is tax deductible seems entirely commonplace. Outside, it's often so quiet that Jackie can hear the sheep chewing in the adjacent meadow as she paints. Up the hill towards the sea, amid the standing stones and lichen-covered rocks, there is a genuine feeling that one might bump into not just the seal pups, hares and herons from Jackie's paintings, but the dragons and fox-riding sprites too. Here, on an average evening, Jackie can be found strolling for inspiration, with her three dogs and some – and just occasionally all – of her six cats.

'Of all God's creatures, there is only one that cannot be

made slave of the leash,' Mark Twain wrote. 'That one is the cat.' Twain said many profound things about felines in his lifetime, but this particular slice of wisdom seems to say less about his knowledge of moggies and more about his lack of exposure to puffins, white rhinos and capybaras. My and Dee's sole attempt attach a lead to Shipley six years previously had led to a kind of voluntary cat paralysis and one of the most impressive Mohicans I'd seen since Howard Jones was in the Top 40. The accompanying stare is not one I have forgotten, and appeared to promise retribution: maybe not today, maybe not tomorrow, but soon, and for the rest of our lives. Yet I've spotted plenty of moggies happily trotting about on leads. Just the day before I arrived at Jackie's place, in a car park just off a Cambridgeshire motorway, I'd seen a Norwegian Forest cat strolling around with its owner, displaying more of a look of haughty squireship than one comes to expect within the boundaries of a Welcome Break service station. Also, I had a fundamental belief, fostered by the long walks I'd undertaken with my childhood cat Monty, that a large number of cats actually liked walking with their humans, especially when there wasn't a lead involved.

Jackie and her cats don't see many people on their walks. 'Most of them say, "Those . . . are cats!" as if they think I haven't noticed,' she told me.

Treleddyd contains less than a dozen houses, perhaps most remarkable of which is that of Jackie's friend Glyn, which, not entirely unlike Glyn himself, looks like it was hewn straight from rock at some point in AD346. Partially blind, 86-year-old Glyn is, according to Jackie, 'the ultimate Cat Man' and has marked out his life in cats with his own moggy graveyard in his back garden. On our way past his house, we met Nadolig, his black and white moggy, whom I estimated to be around two hundred and forty years older than his owner. There is no through-road here, and in the narrow paths that run between the wonky cottages a scattering of dried vole and shrew corpses could be spotted. Essentially, add a few trees made of tuna, and you have Cat Paradise.

Meeting a group of felines for the first time is much like meeting a group of humans in a way: as you spend more time with them, their faces change shape and soften. On first impression, it seems that Jackie owns five identical, smallish ginger cats. Actually, that's incorrect; on first impression, it seems like she owns about *thirty* identical, smallish ginger cats. The truth is she owns four gingers, all of who are related, yet very different. Maurice is the tough guy, slightly standoffish; Pixie and Elmo, his siblings, are very much Jackie's cat ambassadors. That said, Jackie pointed out that Elmo is often led astray and told to do naughty things by an evil doppelganger who looks up at him when he stares into puddles. Martha is, in Jackie's words, 'the matriarch, a storytelling cat'. In my time with Jackie, I failed to hear any of the stories in question, but, noting Martha's dignified aura, I sensed they would be somewhat more poetic and far less profane than the ones Shipley liked to tell me about getting rain on his back and 'nearly knocking out' a massive crow.

The latest addition to Jackie's furry tribe, the sociable and bright-eyed Kiffer, was, on closer inspection, not really ginger at all, but sandy and white, and nowhere near as stupid as he looked. An ear infection in kittenhood meant that he now walked and stalked with his head tilted to one side. This gave him the look of a creature with a compulsion to hunt everything in his path – including, it seemed, me, and a nearby curious heifer. Max, a tabby that Jackie described as 'dark and dangerous' and who has starred in her illustrations for several children's books, is the sole one of her cats who almost never comes on walks.

When Jackie walks with her cats, she tends not to call or whistle them: she simply sets off, and, instinctively realising she is leaving the house, even from the depths of a five-hour nap, they trail along beside her. This is a version of the same telepathy that makes Ralph and Shipley immediately appear in my garden when I go out there, no matter how quietly and surreptitiously I slip out of the house.

'It's always felt very natural to me,' Jackie told me. 'The first time was about twenty years ago, when I lived near Bath, with my old cat Comfrey. I just walked up the hill behind the house and he followed me. He would come to the shops with me.' One element a cat-walker has to be prepared for is the pursuit's unique, stop-start rhythm. As we strolled up the pollen-filled green lane that led from hamlet to the coast, almost all of Jackie's cats dropped off the pace at some point. Maurice was an early straggler. After stalking, then kissing, his bovine friend, Kiffer vanished, not to be seen again for several hours.

Had Kiffer kissed a cow before? 'Oh yes. That happens a lot,' said Jackie. I nodded phlegmatically, surprised at how unsurprised I was. In this fairytale habitat, the idea of a powerful love between cat and cow transcending species limitations and echoing down the years seemed entirely feasible.

A few miles up the coast to the north, we could see the Preseli Hills, where it's said the original stone from Stonehenge came from. Over to our left, in a dip, hid another hamlet, entirely comprising abandoned houses. As we walked to the highest point on the cliff, Jackie told me about a book she was planning about a love affair between two pirates. Had another of my friends, even one who wrote books for a living, told me this, I would have been a little sceptical, but, here, I had no doubt that Jackie could bash the whole thing out in a week or two in a moleskin notebook while sitting on some moss.

'This is my other office,' she said, as we stood on the stones above the sea and Pixie, Elmo and Jackie's three dogs, Bella, Floss and Rosie, sniffed around us. This was a precious, primal, wind-beaten place, a retreat from a retreat. I could feel it soothing me, the sea wind blowing away my worries and keeping at bay the electronic forms of communication that so often seemed to exaggerate them.

As we started back for home, I carried a contented Pixie around my neck for over a mile. It was a mutually beneficial arrangement. Pixie, as Jackie had told me, had been suffering from a cold and wasn't finding it quite as easy to walk as far as normal while, from my point of view, the temperature had dropped, and the girly cotton scarf I'd recently bought from H&M wasn't quite cutting it. But being so close to a ginger cat, being so close to *so many* ginger cats, and their inherent sunny outlook, I could not help being reminded, heartbreakingly, of Pablo. It was looking very much like, in a matter of days, he would no longer be living with me.

Jackie described ginger cats as 'Buddhists, living in the now'. To be frank, it was something of a stretch to picture Pablo kicking off a pair of sandals, lighting a joss stick and getting into the lotus position, but I could partly see what she was getting at. Where my other cats each had their hobbies and plans for the future, Pablo's life was really lived on a moment-to-moment basis. It could be said that Bootsy had a little bit of ginger in her – possibly quite literally, sometimes, if Pablo got his wish – but Pablo was the only one of my cats who had that true ginger sunniness. It could be a good influence on a person, being around that kind of optimism. So often my cats made me feel intellectually inferior, but watching Pablo getting overexcited and self-defeatingly closing the cat food drawer with his paw, forgetting to put his tongue away or doing his Tigger-like bounce into the kitchen and crashing feet-first into a dish full of milk, I had concrete, reassuring proof that I was not the most stupid person in my household. I'd miss that. But then I asked myself a question: 'Which of my cats wouldn't I miss just as much?'

I came up with a giant, gaping blank.

For the last few years of my marriage, without really intend-ing to, I'd relied upon a stock response for the moment when strangers asked me if I had any kids. 'No,' I would tell them. 'Six cats, though!' In all honesty, it was a defence mechanism. I knew all too well how easy it was for a child-less couple in their thirties, who'd been married a few years and had a house full of felines, to be perceived as employing their cats as child substitutes. I viewed the term 'fur babies' about as appealingly as the prospect of eating a tasty pouch from the Sheba Fine Meat Dining Collection, but I had come to the conclusion that I might as well pre-emptively get it out in the open: my domestic life was dominated not by nappies or trips to adventure playgrounds, but by the whims of several furry dictators kind enough to let me share my house with them.

I would not be so presumptuous to claim that dividing

cats in the aftermath of a relationship involves one tenth of the pain that dividing kids in the aftermath of a relationship does, but, in some ways, it at least provides an insight into the latter process. It also marks a similarly painful final curtain to proceedings, an admission that you are at The End, which was another reason Dee and I chose to defer it for some time.

How do two people share between them six animals that they both love to an equal extent? Looking back, it was astonishing to think that at the close of a previous relationship I'd worried about who would get which DVD, book or LP. Put into perspective, next to what was going on now, these matters were immaterial to me: the petty schoolyard concerns of quarter-formed children.

Neither Dee nor I would have liked to think that we had a 'favourite' among our cats but some of the bonds we had with them were undoubtedly more poignant and adhesive than others, and our separation highlighted them, often agonisingly. Bootsy was the cat that we'd got when Dee was ill a few years ago, the cat that, in many ways, helped her recover – the one cat that, even though I was the household's designated Cat Feeder, would always make an unconditional beeline for my wife's lap. I couldn't take her away from Dee, could I? No. But I also found it hard to picture a time when my working days would not feature Bootsy matching me step for step as I paced the house looking for writing inspiration, or trying to muscle her way onto the warm keyboard of my laptop, as she had done almost every day for the last two years while Dee was out at work.

But if Bootsy had to go with Dee, so did Pablo. I'd looked at him as our project cat – the wretch we'd saved from euthanasia who now would happily sleep on my chest without moving for the space of time it took me to read an entire novella – and I wanted to follow the project through, see him continue to gain in confidence. But he and Bootsy were the only two moggies I'd owned who'd ever been inseparable. If I ever needed confirmation, I only had to look at the picture of them in their cat igloo on the cover of the hardback version of my last book; a photograph illustrative of the two ends of the cat intelligence spectrum. It summed up the dynamic of their relationship: the happy idiot and the she-minx who very cleverly made him believe he had her under his control while safe in the knowledge that, all the while, she was calling the shots. Pablo very conveniently served Bootsy's main two wishes in life: to play the puppetmaster, and to be physically worshipped. But Pablo genuinely seemed to *need* Bootsy. She was not only ever so soft and comfortable to sleep on, but fulfilled that shadow carnal need in him left over from when he had balls and strutted his stuff in his free-loving cat commune. And what kind of annihilator of fun would I have been to take that away?

Mostly, our decisions regarding which cat would live with who revolved around more practical concerns. It could be said that, since Dee had owned Janet before she'd met me, perhaps she should have taken him with her. On the other hand, she had the lower income of the two of us, so it would have been unfair of me to expect her to pay the sizable vet bills that were needed to keep his hyperthyroidism at bay. Dee's new house had only a small garden, and it would have been wrong to relocate wanderers such as The Bear, Janet and Shipley from the lush hillside where they lived and foraged to cramped suburbia. And then there was Ralph: in

2001 Dee had handpicked him from the same litter as Shipley – the one cat who could very much be counted as mine from the start, and whose destiny required no lengthy discussion – but he and Pablo were the two cats we most needed to separate.

Do I think the two thirds to one third split we eventually decided upon was fair? No, but only in the sense that I don't think pet custody cases can ever be fair. It was also clear that we had sorted the situation out more amicably than most. During our break-up, a friend of a friend, Steven, told me a story about the two expensive pedigree Bengal cats he and his ex-girlfriend had owned. Steven saw himself as the main cat owner in the couple, chiefly because he had been responsible for nursing one of the Bengals to health when, as a kitten, it had suffered from a rare virus from which his local vet had told him it would not recover. One day, a few weeks after his girlfriend and he had split up, he had got home late at night to his isolated cottage after being away on a business trip and found that she had been back and taken both cats. That had been over a year ago, and he hadn't seen either cat, or his ex, since.

Perhaps the one area of contention might have been The Bear: a cat that had been Dee's companion since she was nineteen. Some might have assumed we'd end up in a court-room with him, each of us, unbeknown to the other, hiding Tesco Finest Shetland Isles Smoked Salmon in the lining of our jackets in order to convince a judge that we were more worthy of The Bear's affection. In truth, there was very little to debate. This was not fundamentally about Dee's greater history with The Bear, the fact that he had once been her former boyfriend's favourite cat, or about her frequent claim to me that 'he likes you better'. It was mostly about the fact that neither of us wanted this survivor cat – this veteran of fourteen house moves – to have the trauma of moving again.

Once, early during my attempt to catch Winston the stray, I'd gone out to check the trap, and been elated to find him in there, disorientation all over his muzzle. A bigger surprise came when I realised that his enormous, ugly neck wound had completely healed. It had taken almost a full minute before I realised that I was actually looking at The Bear, and, by mistaking him for Winston, I'd momentarily been able to see him through the eyes of an outsider, and realise his true plump, lavish healthiness. The rejuvenating effect that five and a half years of being in the same place had had on him was plain and radiant to see.

Over the following months, I would occasionally visit Pablo and Bootsy, and Dee would report back to me on how they were settling in to their new home. They had been thrust into a far less rural habitat, but it was a cat-friendly one nonetheless. I knew this from two frustratedly catless friends in the area, Drew and Jecca, who had set up their own 'Cat Stock Market' on the Internet in order to keep track of the ups and downs of the endless moggies who visited their garden, including the mighty Gingersaurus and the near-iconic Crybaby Hedge Cat, a creature I'd sadly never crossed paths with on my visits to the area and who sounded, from all descriptions, like Ralph's lost soulmate.

Not that Bootsy and Pablo's world of two allowed for much furry networking. Their relationship had reached a new, intimate intensity, the highs and lows of their dry humping sessions respectively higher and lower than ever before, their post-semi-coital cuddling now undisturbed by the malicious whims of Ralph and Shipley. Due to the lack of space outdoors and an evil tortoiseshell cat that liked to stare in through the window at her, Bootsy had taken to emptying her bowels in Dee's fresh laundry pile, leading Dee to succumb to the purchase of a litter tray. Pablo himself had refrained from exploiting this but in a spirit of generosity, perhaps to atone for all the times he had bitten her neck overzealously while frotting with her, would follow Bootsy into the litter and bury her wares for her.

Perhaps even more eccentric was Pablo and Bootsy's new drinking regime. Both had always been fussy drinkers, in their own personal ways. Bootsy, while stopping slightly short of demanding her own water filter, liked to have the cold tap in the kitchen slowly dribbled in order to get the water at its freshest, while Pablo's preferred receptacle was a glass that had been placed in the sink the night before. Now, walking into Dee's kitchen, I noticed a full water glass in the cats' drinking bowl. 'It's the only thing that seems to work,' she told me. 'I'm hoping it might encourage them.'

When I arrived, Pablo still bounded towards me as soon as I came in through the front door, but Pablo would probably have bounded towards Hannibal Lecter if he'd also come in through the front door. In Bootsy, by contrast, I could see genuine recognition, and critical appraisal. I thought I saw a hint of the resentment of the unfairly abandoned, but Bootsy had never been a fan of facial hair, and any shrinking away from me she did was probably just a reaction to my latest beard. After fifteen minutes, she'd thaw out, and then, when it was time to leave, I'd find it hard to prise her off my chest. I could have really milked it, claimed this was evidence that she obviously couldn't bear to let me go, but the truth was that she'd always had trouble retracting her claws.

Back at The Upside Down House, I was noticing changes in my cats too, many of them arguably less subtle. The Bear's contentedness had now become so extreme it could, in a certain light, have been looked upon as smug, and he had been experimenting with a new 'advert dog' head movement during the times he caught me alone in the kitchen: a slight tilt of the chin, coupled with widened eyes, followed by a just-perceptible nod towards the food drawer. Ralph certainly seemed happier for Pablo's absence, but I wondered if his war against ginger had defined his reason for existing for so long that he felt like half a cat without it. My hopes that he would stop shouting 'RALPH!' outside the window at five in the morning had come to fruition, but only for him to begin shouting 'HELLO!' outside the window at five in the morning instead. This was impressive enough, something I could boast about to friends, but in the end it was a little like the man on the other side of the lake who swore at the ducks: on the four hundredth listen, the eccentricity started to peel away, and you started to realise that you were just hearing the sound of someone going about, what to them, was the fundamental, mundane business of the day. We all had a job to do. In my case, that meant sitting in front of a computer and writing. In Ralph's case, it meant repeatedly shouting oddly human greetings at the top of his voice until someone came outside and gently nudged him in the direction of the cat flap while calling him an irritating cock puppet. It wasn't much of a living, but someone had to do it.

When I'd lived with Dee, I had always been the person the cats had harassed most fervently for food and attention, but I was not imagining it when I noticed that, without her there, they began to redouble their efforts to gang up on me. I have no idea what tipped the balance. It wasn't as if Dee acted like a Victorian schoolmistress with them; she'd simply been better than me at ignoring them when they were at their most demanding. Did they see a hint of defeat in my eyes? Or was it a kind of natural selection: the strong preying on the weak, as they have done in animal and human life for time immemorial? Whatever the case, without Dee there, they had never been so loud and demonstrative regarding their needs.

Sometimes, I got the sense that Janet and Shipley had got together and decided that, if they tried hard enough, they could physically bat me from my study on the ground floor all the way up two flights of stairs to the fridge. I had always thought 'ankle biter' was a term exclusively applied to dogs and small children until Shipley began obsessively following me around the house in late 2009. 'How would one go about putting a restraining order on one's own cat?' I wondered to myself, as, in the midst of a conversation with the postman, I felt a pinch and looked down to find a small black muzzle fastened neatly yet insistently onto the bottom of my leg.

Of course, one advantage of having four, instead of six, cats is that there are marginally fewer cleaning duties to perform. Pablo and Bootsy were champion shedders and sometimes when I missed watching Pablo hooking a paw into the back of the biscuit dispenser or the ballet of a Bootsy jump up to the arm of the sofa, I could at least try to convince myself that there was compensation in now once again owning two dark blue sofas, instead of one orange one and one grey one. Despite this, I continued to employ a cleaner for two hours a week.

When I tell people I pay someone to clean my house, I always hear the same voice in my head. It's not the voice of anyone specific, more an amalgam of that of old, forgotten school friends and elder family members who grew up in poverty. What the voice says can be clearly discerned as 'OOH, get *you*' but it actually sounds more like an insistent, piercing fire alarm of the kind that might wake you in the middle of the night in a hotel room and lead to some kind of embarrassing naked episode. Despite the voice's disapproval, every Monday, when my cleaner, Melissa, leaves, I feel purged and secure in the sense that I have fought off a nightmare future vision of cat ownership for another week. Quite simply, a small amount of professional cleaning feels to me like a mandatory part of not becoming the super villain known as Bad Multiple Cat Owner. This has been pretty much the case since the day in 2005 when The Bear was going through one of his darker phases, and Dee and I used a UV light to perform a rather troubling forensic examination of the substances on our curtains and cupboards.

Melissa has been working for me for eighteen months now, and with that comes a certain pride. I might not have successfully sustained a relationship, but I am, finally, finding the formula to successfully sustain a cleaner: something I've found surprisingly hard in the past. I know Elaine loved my cats and left only because she retired, and, for Grace, cleaning was just a stopgap between other jobs, but Valerie, who simply did not turn up one week and was never heard from again, remains a mystery. As for Michelle, the company she worked for told me she'd left to pursue 'other options', but I can't help thinking back to the packet of condoms Dee and I once left out by mistake on cleaning day. And as regards the handcuffs on the kitchen table the following week, the truth is that they were a promotional item, sent by a DVD company promoting a police-themed TV show I was reviewing for a newspaper, and I never even troubled to unlock – let alone use – them. I suppose, though, that Michelle wasn't to realise that. Who knows? Perhaps she simply got a better job, or didn't like cats, but I do wonder if Gay Talese's book *Love Thy Neighbour's Wife* might have had just a little to do with it. It's really a very intellectual and sober examination into the 70s' sex industry, but a person might not necessarily assume that from the racy cover of my paperback copy of it. I hadn't really thought twice about leaving it open on the bed, but arriving back home and seeing that it had been tidied to the bedside table, and remembering that the handcuff episode was still fresh in the memory, I began to re-evaluate my decision not to put it out of sight.

I don't leave my collection of 1970s *Playboys* lying around when Melissa cleans and, even if I did, I doubt I'd feel the need to explain that I read them for the high standard of investigative journalism and short fiction within. Also, I know Melissa likes cats – none more so than Janet. The two of them have cultivated a close and rather unique bond over the last year and a half. When she arrives, she will go and find him, and scruff his chest: his favourite manner of being stroked, ever since his heart began to murmur. Then he will follow her around as she cleans, inspecting her work. Most cats are scared of vacuum cleaners, but Janet views Melissa's as an opponent more than an enemy, and, in order to vanquish it, he will leave large clumps of fur in the exact places it has just cleaned.

I'll generally tidy up quite thoroughly for Melissa before she arrives, and carry out a thorough vole scan, but sometimes, during her two hours here, Shipley and Ralph will leave her little offerings. As someone raised deep in the countryside, Melissa is not fazed by these. Sometimes, she will tell me about the ferret one of her friends keeps near-permanently in his pocket, or her early childhood, living in a house with two dogs and a fox called Penny that her dad had found abandoned as a cub and raised as a canine. Hearing these stories, I'll realise how fundamentally unadventurous I am as an animal owner, and begin to get ideas. 'How easy,' I muse to myself, 'would it be to transport a goat down the spiral staircase outside my bedroom?' Or: 'When people say that, in owning donkeys, a person can never keep just one donkey, and must keep a donkey pal to keep the first donkey company, do they exclusively mean " donkey" when referring to the second donkey, or do they actually also mean "cat with some extremely donkeyish aspects"?'

Despite not having the rational voice of Dee around to tell me why I can't follow through on any of these ideas, I've surprised myself with my self-restraint. For now, instead of filling the house with animals, I've filled it with people.

I always used to think I was very bad at hosting parties. I would get too worried that I wouldn't get to speak to everyone there, too concerned that everyone was having a good time, but recently, I seem to have got myself on a good run. I still have more than my share of neglectful moments as a host. I probably should have told the comedian who stayed at my house that I had four cats before, without the help of Piriton, he spent a wheezing sleepless night here, rendering himself ill-prepared for his spoken-word event in Norwich the following day. Also, looking back, leaving thirty leftover chicken wings on the dining table, uncovered, overnight, with four sets of whiskers in close quarters, while guests slept on the same floor, was something of an oversight.

I also have a lodger now, Katia. She's a Dog Person, but seems to be coming round to cats – especially now she has realised the fundamental rule that, in a house containing four of them, it's best not to walk across a room barefooted in the dark. There are also signs that she is starting to gain a fundamental understanding of mine. 'I've started to realise,' she told me recently, 'Ralph is like the guy I fancy, but The Bear is the guy I *love*. The other two are cats.'

I have done my best to make this house my own, but there have been times when everything in it has seemed to lead me back to Dee. Beyond the décor we chose together and the remnants of the furniture we bought, I have walking reminders of us around me on a daily basis, and even they bring their own, other, half-walking reminders: the moorhen that I chased around the room that made me think of its predecessor whose legs the two of us found sticking out comically from behind the sofa when it was 'having a rest' from a somewhat Benny Hill-style chasing episode with Pablo and Shipley; the heartbreaking teenage rat Shipley maimed, which reduced me to tears even before it reminded me of the story Dee had told me about Dylan, the rat she used to keep as a teenager, which would pick up a tiny brush between its teeth and bring it to her so she could stroke him with it. Inevitably the passing of time will make me – is making me – miss her less than I once did, but in my cats I have a lasting connection to her. When I answer people's questions about them, she is an indelible part of the story. There is, after all, no way to explain that one of your cats was your ex's ex's favourite pet, without mentioning your ex.

I sometimes start answering one of these questions with the word 'We . . .', then check myself for a moment, having an instinct to change it to 'I . . .' At the time, my house will frequently have various people milling round it. Downstairs, my new lodger Katia will be telling a guest about Ralph's sideburns. In the kitchen, four or five conversations might be going on at once, and in the midst of them might be found Shipley, concerned about not being the loudest individual in the room and making his yapping, swearing demands like some kind of proletarian Siamese with Tourette's syndrome. It's unlikely The Bear will be around, but just occasionally he might be spotted looking deep into the eyes of a rare melancholy guest, or surveying the room from beneath the stairs, while perched on top of his Kitty Boutique Disco Scratching Pole. Janet will often not be far away – either suffering from the debilitating condition known as 'sour cream chin' having raided the dips, or playing a game of 'Prison' with a couple of guests between the bars of the stairs. I'll look around for a moment, considering my options. The word 'we' does feel odd on my tongue, and my throat catches as I play around with it. But would it be a lie, or a complete delusion, to use it in these circumstances? I decide it wouldn't.

Then, pressing forward, I'll tell the story.